HOUGHTON MIFFLIN HARCOURT

FLORIDA
JOURNEYS
COMMON CORE

Program Authors

James F. Baumann · David J. Chard · Jamal Cooks · J. David Cooper · Russell Gersten · Marjorie Lipson
Lesley Mandel Morrow · John J. Pikulski · Héctor H. Rivera · Mabel Rivera · Shane Templeton · Sheila W. Valencia
Catherine Valentino · MaryEllen Vogt

Consulting Author
Irene Fountas

Printed in the U.S.A.

ISBN 978-0-547-86080-0

5 6 7 8 9 - 0868 – 21 20 19 18 17 16 15 14 13
4500420147   C D E F G

HOUGHTON MIFFLIN HARCOURT

Unit 1

Unit 2

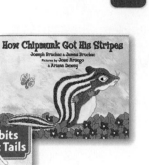

Poppleton in Winter
FANTASY
by Cynthia Rylant • illustrated by Mark Teague

Welcome, Reader!

You are about to begin a journey into reading. Along the way you will meet many new characters, such as a superhero dog. You'll also travel under the sea and to many other exciting places. Your journey is sure to be filled with surprises. You will learn to be a better reader, too!

Get ready to meet some new friends with the story *Henry and Mudge*. Turn the page and let the fun begin!

Sincerely,

The Authors

Unit 1

HENRY AND MUDGE
The First Book
Story by Cynthia Rylant
Pictures by Suçie Stevenson

All in the Family

☑ TARGET VOCABULARY

curly
straight
floppy
drooled
weighed
stood
collars
row

Vocabulary
Reader

Pet
Rabbits

Context
Cards

COMMON
CORE

LACC.2.L.3.6 use words and phrases acquired
through conversations, reading and being read to,
and responding to texts

Go
Digital

10

Vocabulary in Context

▶ Read each **Context Card**.

▶ Use a **Vocabulary** word to tell about something you did.

1
curly
A poodle is a dog that has very curly hair.

2
straight
Some kinds of dogs have long, straight hair.

③ floppy

Hound dogs have floppy ears. The ears hang down very low.

④ drooled

The Saint Bernard drooled all over the place!

⑤ weighed

A dog can be weighed on a scale. Then the vet knows how heavy the dog is.

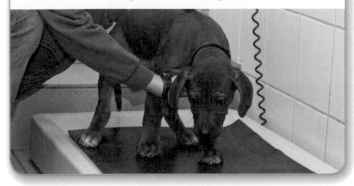

⑥ stood

The children measured the dog. He stood one foot tall.

⑦ collars

Collars come in different styles. A collar goes around a dog's neck.

⑧ row

The dog treats are lined up in a row on the shelf.

Read and Comprehend

 **Go Digital**

☑ **TARGET SKILL**

Sequence of Events In *Henry and Mudge,* one event happens and then another and another. The order of events in a story is called the **sequence of events.** You can use a chart like this one to show the order of story events.

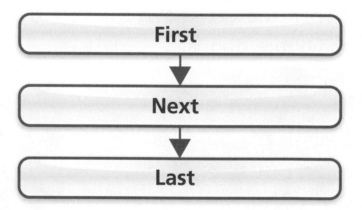

First

↓

Next

↓

Last

☑ **TARGET STRATEGY**

Infer/Predict Use clues, or text evidence, to figure out more about story parts.

COMMON CORE **LACC.2.RL.1.2** recount stories and determine their message, lesson, or moral; **LACC.2.RL.2.5** describe the overall structure of a story

Animal Traits

All dogs are alike in some ways. Dogs are also different in some ways. Some dogs are short. Some dogs are tall. Some have long, skinny tails. Some have short, fluffy tails. The different ways a dog can look are called traits. Each dog's traits make it special.

In *Henry and Mudge,* you will read about one dog who looks different from all the others.

13

ANCHOR TEXT

✓ TARGET SKILL

Sequence of Events

Tell the order in which things happen.

✓ GENRE

Realistic fiction is a story that could happen in real life. As you read, look for:

▸ characters who act like real people

▸ story events that could happen to you or to someone you know

COMMON CORE LACC.2.RL.1.2 recount stories and determine their message, lesson, or moral; **LACC.2.RL.2.4** describe how words and phrases supply rhythm and meaning; **LACC.2.RL.2.5** describe the overall structure of a story; **LACC.2.RL.4.10** read and comprehend literature

MEET THE AUTHOR
Cynthia Rylant

Henry and Mudge have starred in more than twenty-five books by Cynthia Rylant. A musical based on their adventures once toured the United States. The part of Mudge was played by a grown man in a dog costume!

MEET THE ILLUSTRATOR
Suçie Stevenson

Suçie Stevenson loves drawing the character of Mudge. In fact, she has two big dogs of her own. "They don't drool as much as Mudge," she says.

HENRY and MUDGE

by Cynthia Rylant

illustrated by Suçie Stevenson

ESSENTIAL QUESTION

What is a perfect
pet like?

Henry had no brothers and no sisters.
"I want a brother," he told his parents.
"Sorry," they said.
Henry had no friends on his street.

"I want to live on a different street,"
he told his parents.
"Sorry," they said.
Henry had no pets at home.
"I want to have a dog," he told his parents.
"Sorry," they *almost* said.

But first they looked at their house
with no brothers and sisters.
Then they looked at their street
with no children.
Then they looked at Henry's face.

Then they looked at each other.
"Okay," they said.
"I want to hug you!" Henry told
his parents.
And he did.

ANALYZE THE TEXT

Sequence of Events What
happens after Henry's parents
look at each other?

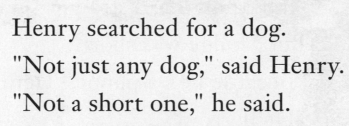

Henry searched for a dog.
"Not just any dog," said Henry.
"Not a short one," he said.
"Not a curly one," he said.
"And no pointed ears."

Then he found Mudge.

Mudge had floppy ears, not pointed.

And Mudge had straight fur, not curly.

But Mudge was short.

"Because he's a puppy," Henry said.

"He'll grow."

ANALYZE THE TEXT

Author's Word Choice What words does the author use to describe Mudge?

And did he ever!

He grew out of his puppy cage.

He grew out of his dog cage.

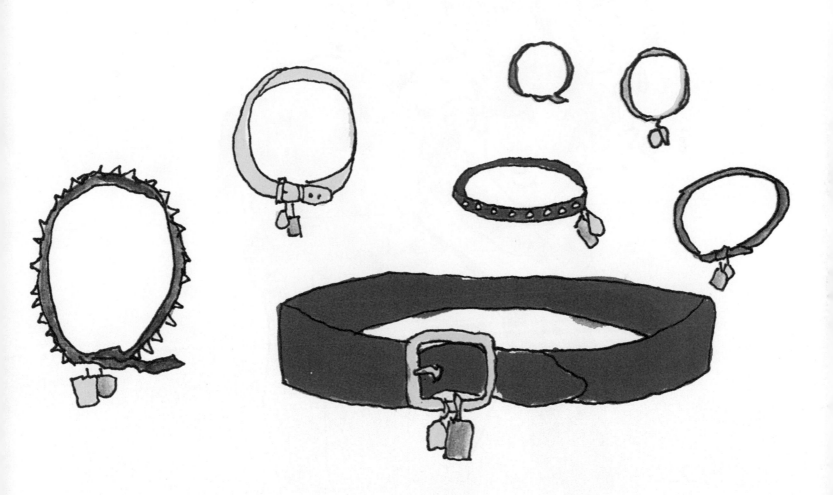

He grew out of seven collars in a row.

And when he finally stopped growing . . .

he weighed
one hundred eighty pounds,
he stood three feet tall,
and he drooled.
"I'm glad you're not short,"
Henry said.
And Mudge licked him,
then sat on him.

Dig Deeper

How to Analyze the Text

Use these pages to learn about Sequence of Events and Author's Word Choice. Then read *Henry and Mudge* again. Use what you learn to understand it better.

Sequence of Events

In *Henry and Mudge,* you read about how Henry's family gets Mudge. The author writes about what happens in a certain order. The order of what happens in a story is called the **sequence of events.**

Think about what happens first, next, and last in the story. You can show sequence of events in a chart like the one below.

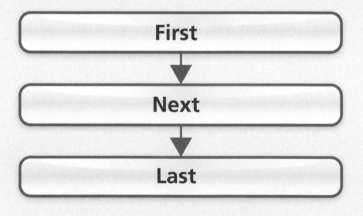

 LACC.2.RL.1.2 recount stories and determine their message, lesson, or moral; **LACC.2.RL.2.4** describe how words and phrases supply rhythm and meaning; **LACC.2.RL.2.5** describe the overall structure of a story

Author's Word Choice

Authors think about which words and phrases to use in a story. Choosing strong words makes the story interesting. Some strong words can help you picture what is happening and what things look like. As you reread the story, think about the words the author uses to tell about Mudge.

Your Turn

 Turn and Talk

What is a perfect pet like? Talk about your ideas with a partner. Take turns talking. Use text evidence from *Henry and Mudge* to tell your ideas. Listen carefully to what your partner says, and ask questions if you don't understand something.

Classroom Conversation

Now talk about these questions with the class.

1. Why did Henry want a dog?

2. What happens as Mudge grows? Find text evidence to explain. Use the words and pictures to tell what happens in order.

3. Do you think Henry and his parents knew how big Mudge would get? Why or why not?

WRITE ABOUT READING

Response Think about what Henry asks for at the beginning of the story. Do you think that Henry's parents are right to let him get a dog? Write a few sentences to explain your opinion. Use text evidence from the story to help tell your reasons.

Writing Tip

Use a capital letter at the beginning of each sentence. Use an end mark at the end of each sentence.

COMMON CORE **LACC.2.RL.3.7** use information from illustrations and words to demonstrate understanding of characters, setting, or plot; **LACC.2.W.1.1** write opinion pieces; **LACC.2.SL.1.1.a** follow rules for discussions

INFORMATIONAL TEXT

All in the Family

☑ GENRE

Informational text gives facts about a topic.

☑ TEXT FOCUS

Headings are titles for different parts of a selection.

 Go Digital

All in the Family

by Katherine Mackin

At the San Antonio Zoo, you can see many amazing animals. Some of these animals may have a family member living in your neighborhood!

Different Kinds of **Dogs**

Bush dogs live in Central America and South America. They have straight, brown fur. In the wild, they eat large rodents.

Pet dogs come in all shapes and sizes. They may have floppy ears or curly hair. They eat food made for dogs. Pet dogs should wear collars.

Cats of All Sizes

Lions belong to the cat family. They can grow up to eight feet long. Some have stood four feet tall. Lions hunt big animals in the wild.

Most house cats do not weigh more than fifteen pounds. They mostly eat special food for cats. However, some cats like to hunt for mice or birds.

Large Lizards

Komodo dragons are the largest lizards. They can grow to ten feet long. Some have weighed five hundred pounds! The saliva of a Komodo dragon is dangerous. You would not want to be drooled on by a Komodo dragon!

Little Lizards

Geckos belong to the lizard family. They are about eight inches long. Adult geckos weigh about one to two ounces. Geckos eat insects. They can eat ten crickets in a row.

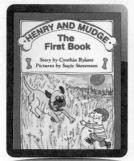

Compare Texts

Compare and Contrast With a partner, pick one of the animals from *All in the Family*. Discuss how that animal is the same as and different from Mudge. Ask questions if you don't understand something your partner says.

Make a List Henry convinces his parents to get a dog. What reasons does he give? Imagine you want a new pet. List your reasons.

Connect to Science Choose an animal from *All in the Family* to research. Make a list of questions and find the answers. Then share the answers with a partner.

 LACC.2.RI.3.9 compare and contrast points presented by two texts on same topic; **LACC.2.W.3.8** recall information from experiences or gather information to answer a question

Grammar

Subjects and Predicates The **subject** of a sentence is the naming part. It tells who or what did or does something.

Pam walks her dog.
The boy chooses a pet.

The **predicate** of a sentence is the action part. It tells what the subject did or does.

The dogs pull on a rope.
Ben plays with his dog.

 **Write each sentence. Then circle the subject.**

❶ Mel grew tall.

❷ My father hugs the dog.

Write each sentence. Draw a line under the predicate.

❶ The boys play ball.

❷ Susan fed her dog.

When two short sentences have the same predicate, you can put the sentences together. Join them to make one longer sentence. Write *and* between the two subjects. This will make your writing smoother.

Short Sentences

Jim liked the park.

Spot liked the park.

New Sentence with Joined Subjects

Jim and Spot liked the park.

📓 Connect Grammar to Writing

When you revise your sentences, try joining sentences that have the same predicate.

Narrative Writing

 Ideas Use details when you write a **true story** about something that happened. Details help your reader picture what you are telling about.

Megan drafted some sentences for a true story. See how she revised her writing to add details.

Writing Traits Checklist

✓ **Ideas**
Did I use details to tell the reader more?

✓ **Organization**
Did I tell about events in an order that makes sense?

✓ **Word Choice**
Did I use words that describe?

✓ **Voice**
Does my writing sound like the way I would tell the story?

Revised Draft

My friend Lucy gave me a beautiful ^ bracelet. with many colorful beads She made it. She ^ calls it a friendship bracelet.

When I wear it I think of my

best friend Lucy. ^

I love my bracelet!

A Gift

by Megan Stiles

My friend Lucy gave me a beautiful bracelet. She made it with many colorful beads. She calls it a friendship bracelet. When I wear it I think of my best friend Lucy. I love my bracelet!

Reading as a Writer

How do the words that Megan added help you picture what she is telling about? Where can you add details to your true story?

I added details to my final paper to make it more interesting.

2

☑ TARGET VOCABULARY

remembered

porch

crown

spend

stuck

visit

cousin

piano

Vocabulary Reader

Context Cards

LACC.2.L.3.6 use words and phrases acquired through conversations, reading and being read to, and responding to texts

Vocabulary in Context

► Read each **Context Card.**

► Place the Vocabulary words in alphabetical order.

---

1 **remembered**

Mom remembered my birthday. She never forgets.

---

2 **porch**

They sat outside and talked on the front porch.

3 crown

This girl wears a crown on her head for her birthday.

4 spend

These girls spend time together. They play every day.

5 stuck

While on vacation, their car got stuck in the mud. It can't move.

6 visit

These grandparents like to visit. They see their grandchildren a lot.

7 cousin

My aunt and uncle have three children. Each child is my cousin.

8 piano

The father teaches his child to play the piano, a musical instrument.

Read and Comprehend

Compare and Contrast In *My Family*, you will find out how the people in a family are alike and different. When you think about how things are alike, you **compare** them. When you think about how things are different, you **contrast** them. You can use a diagram like this one to show how things are alike and different.

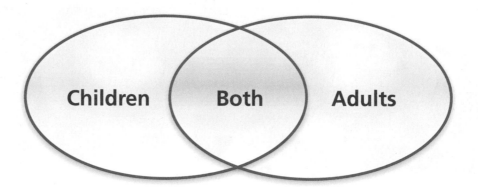

Question Ask questions about what you are reading.

Family Time

Families spend time together. They can do many different things. Some families play board games. Some families like to go to the zoo. Others enjoy playing outside. Sometimes families make and eat dinner together. What does your family like to do together?

My Family is about a girl named Camila. You will read about what she likes to do with her family.

Lesson 2

ANCHOR TEXT

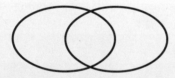

MEET THE AUTHOR AND PHOTOGRAPHER

George Ancona

George Ancona is often asked if he keeps in touch with the people he photographs. The answer is yes! Not long ago, he heard from the father of the young boy he had photographed for *Pablo Remembers*. Pablo, now grown, was getting married. Mr. Ancona went back to Mexico to go to Pablo's wedding!

My Family

by George Ancona

ESSENTIAL QUESTION

What are some things
that families like to
do together?

I am Camila. I live in Miami with my
mother, Damaris, my father, Roberto, and my
brother, René. My mother came from Cuba.
My father came from Puerto Rico.

My mother and I go to school together.
That's because she teaches Spanish in my
school. When we are at home, I like to help
her cook dinner.

Sometimes when my Grandma Marta comes to visit, I dress up and put on a show for her. Today she is teaching me a song. It goes like this:

There once was a sailor at sea
who liked to play the guitar.
When he remembered his far away land
he picked his guitar, and started to sing:
On the high sea, on the high sea, on the
high sea. [repeat]

René is my little brother. Our friends and
family come to the house for his birthday. We play
games, eat, and sing "Happy Birthday" to him.

Here is my family: Grandmother Marta and Grandfather Rigoberto had four children. Almost all of them came to René's birthday party.

Marta & Rigoberto

| Andrés & Darleen | María Irene & Victor | Martica & Miguel | Damaris & Roberto | ◀ They married: |

| Victor Mar Isabel | Victoria Valeria Vanesa | Gabriela Leticia | René Camila | And they had these children: ◀ |

49

Grandma came with Aunt María Irene and Victoria. Uncle Andrés came with Victor and Mar Isabel. Aunt Martica, Uncle Miguel, Gabriela, and Leticia came too. Soon the house was full.

We played many games. Aunt María Irene showed us how to play hopscotch. Little Leticia put on a crown to dance. Grandpa Rigoberto danced with cousin Mar Isabel.

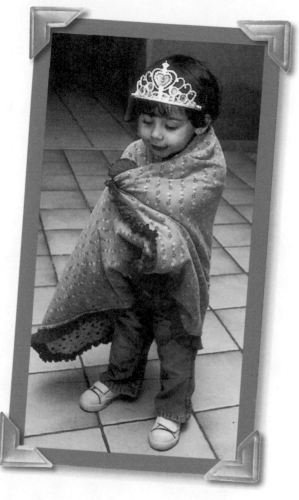

ANALYZE THE TEXT

Genre: Informational Text
What do you learn about Camila's family from the photos?

51

On Sundays we go to church with Grandma.
Then we all go to Aunt Martica and Uncle Miguel's
house. After lunch we play music and sing.

Uncle Miguel plays the double bass. Uncle
Andrés plays the violin. Aunt Darleen plays the
piano. Victor plays the clarinet and Mar Isabel
plays the flute.

We spend the rest of the day in the
backyard. The grown-ups play dominoes while
Uncle Andrés tells funny stories. Gabriela and I
sit on the porch and paint pictures.

ANALYZE THE TEXT

Compare and Contrast How are
the activities of the adults the same
as and different from the activities
of the children on this page?

What I like best is when Papi takes us fishing. Most of the time my hook gets stuck on a rock. I can't wait to catch my first fish.

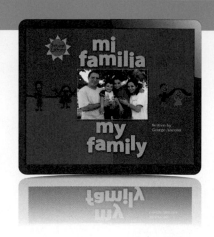

Dig Deeper

How to Analyze the Text

Use these pages to learn about Compare and Contrast and Informational Text. Then read *My Family* again. Use what you learn to understand it better.

Compare and Contrast

In *My Family*, you read about the people in Camila's family. You can **compare** the people in her family by thinking about how they are alike. You can **contrast** them by thinking about how they are different.

Comparing and contrasting can help you understand more about people or ideas. Use a diagram like this one to compare and contrast the children and adults in Camila's family.

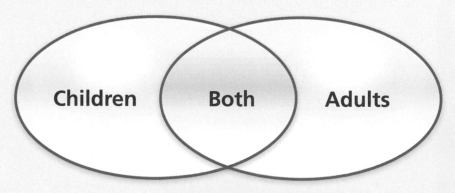

 LACC.2.RI.1.1 ask and answer questions to demonstrate understanding of key details; **LACC.2.RI.3.7** explain how images contribute to and clarify text

Genre: Informational Text

The author of an **informational text** tells real information about a topic. Informational text often has photos instead of illustrations. Authors choose photos that tell more about the topic. You can use photos to get more information than you find in the words. Look at page 46. The photos show that Camila is happy to sing the song that Grandma Marta teaches her.

Your Turn

RETURN TO THE ESSENTIAL QUESTION

 What are some things that families like to do together? Discuss your ideas with a partner. Use text evidence from *My Family* to explain. Take turns talking, and listen carefully when it is your partner's turn to speak.

 Classroom Conversation

Now talk about these questions with the class.

1. How are the mother and father in the family the same and different?

2. How does the family tree help you understand Camila's family?

3. What parts of the selection tell you that Camila has a large family?

Response Write about how you think Camila and her family feel about spending time together. Use the words and photos to give text evidence for your answer.

Writing Tip

Make sure that each sentence has a subject and a predicate.

COMMON CORE **LACC.2.RI.1.1** ask and answer questions to demonstrate understanding of key details; **LACC.2.W.1.1** write opinion pieces; **LACC.2.SL.1.1.a** follow rules for discussions

POETRY

Family Poetry

Family Poetry

A family may have parents, brothers, sisters, grandparents, cousins, and more. People in a family visit one another and spend time together. Poets write about these remembered times. Listen to the rhythm of these family poems as you read them.

Everybody Says

Everybody says

I look just like my mother.

Everybody says

I'm the image of Aunt Bee.

Everybody says

My nose is like my father's.

But *I* want to look like ME!

by Dorothy Aldis

 LACC.2.RL.2.4 describe how words and phrases supply rhythm and meaning; LACC.2.RL.4.10 read and comprehend literature

Abuelita's Lap

I know a place where I can sit
and tell about my day,
tell every color that I saw
from green to cactus gray.

I know a place where I can sit
and hear a favorite beat,
her heart and *cuentos* from the past,
the rhythms honey-sweet.

I know a place where I can sit
and listen to a star,
listen to its silent song
gliding from afar.

I know a place where I can sit
and hear the wind go by,
hearing it spinning round my house,
my whirling lullaby.

by Pat Mora

Grandpa's Stories

The pictures on the television
Do not make me dream as well
As the stories without pictures
Grandpa knows how to tell.

Even if he does not know
What makes a Spaceman go,
Grandpa says back in his time
Hamburgers only cost a dime,
Ice cream cones a nickel,
And a penny for a pickle.

by Langston Hughes

Write a Family Poem

What do you like to do with your family?
Do you tell stories on the porch?
Do you play the piano and sing?
Write a poem about your family.
Use words and phrases that give
your poem rhythm.

Compare Texts

Select a Poem Which poem from *Family Poetry* do you think Camila would say best tells about her family? Share your ideas with a partner.

Select an Activity Think about what Camila and her family do in *My Family*. Which of these activities would you like to do with a family member? Tell why.

Connect to Social Studies Camila's mother came from Cuba. Her father came from Puerto Rico. Now her family lives in Miami. With a partner, find these places on a map. Talk about where you could look to find out more about these places.

LACC.2.RI.1.1 ask and answer questions to demonstrate understanding of key details

65

Grammar

Complete Simple Sentences A complete **simple sentence** has both a **subject** and a **predicate.** The subject tells who or what did or does something. The predicate tells what the subject did or does.

Subject	Predicate
Ana	sings.
My older brother	plays the drums.

Try This! **Work with a partner. Read each group of words aloud. Tell which groups of words are sentences.**

❶ Dad cooked.

❷ Harry's birthday.

❸ Ate three slices of cake!

❹ Jen and Bobbi danced.

When you write, use complete sentences. Be sure that simple sentences have a subject and a predicate.

Not Complete Simple Sentences

My family.

Was Auntie Lu's birthday.

Complete Simple Sentences

My family had a party. It was Auntie Lu's birthday.

 Connect Grammar to Writing

When you revise your friendly letter, fix any sentences that are not complete. Add a subject or a predicate.

Narrative Writing

☑ **Voice** When you write a **friendly letter,** the voice of your letter shows what you are like.

Nestor drafted a letter to his uncle. Then he added words to make the letter sound more like the way he would talk to his uncle.

Writing Traits Checklist

☑ **Organization**
Did I use the five parts of a friendly letter? Did I tell things in order?

☑ **Word Choice**
Did I use words that tell how I feel?

☑ **Voice**
Does the letter sound like me?

☑ **Conventions**
Did I capitalize and punctuate the date, greeting, and closing correctly?

Revised Draft

Dear Uncle Julio,

We had fun at Grandma

Rita's last Sunday. We played
my favorite
∧ games. Auntie Selena sang.

Hector played his guitar.

those songs that you and
I used to sing together

68

September 24, 2015

Dear Uncle Julio,

    We had fun at Grandma Rita's last Sunday. We played my favorite games. Auntie Selena sang those songs that you and I used to sing together. Hector played his guitar. I wish you had been there. Maybe you can come the next time we go to Grandma Rita's. I miss you!

Love,
Nestor

Reading as a Writer

What did Nestor add to let you know how he feels? What can you add to your letter to show your thoughts and feelings?

I added words so my letter sounds like me and shows how I feel.

Dogs
by Jennifer Blitzin Gillis

Helping Paws

✓ **TARGET VOCABULARY**

hairy

mammals

litter

stayed

canned

chews

clipped

coat

Vocabulary Reader

Pets at the Vet

Context Cards

LACC.2.L.3.6 use words and phrases acquired through conversations, reading and being read to, and responding to texts

Go Digital

Vocabulary in Context

▶ Read each **Context Card**.

▶ Talk about a picture. Use a different Vocabulary word from the one on the card.

1 hairy

This dog is very hairy. It has a lot of long fur.

2 mammals

Cats are mammals, but fish are not.

3 litter

These puppies are different colors, but they are from the same litter.

4 stayed

My dog stayed at my cousin's house while we were on vacation.

5 canned

This man chose canned dog food at the pet store.

6 chews

My older brother gets upset when our puppy chews on his shoes!

7 clipped

The lost dog had a name tag clipped to her collar. It helped us find her owner.

8 coat

This fox has a thick coat that helps it keep warm in the winter.

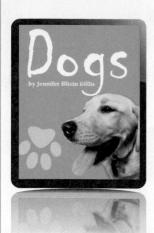

Dogs
by Jennifer Blizin Gillis

Read and Comprehend

Go Digital

Author's Purpose An author may write for different reasons. The reason an author writes a selection is called the **author's purpose**. An author's purpose may be to explain something. It could also be to tell a story or to make the reader laugh.

Use text evidence as clues to help you figure out why an author wrote something. You can use a chart like this one to help you.

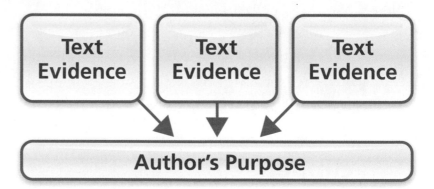

| Text Evidence | Text Evidence | Text Evidence |

Author's Purpose

Analyze/Evaluate Think about the details as you read. Then tell how you decided which details are important.

Animal Traits

Different kinds of pets have different traits. A trait tells something about the way a pet looks or acts. Pets need different kinds of care depending on their traits. For example, a pet cat might have long fur. That cat's owner must brush the fur often. A pet fish lives in water. A fish owner must make sure the water is clean.

Dogs is about having a pet dog. You will read about how to take care of that kind of pet.

ANCHOR TEXT

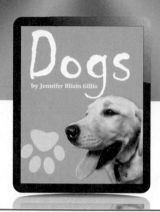

✓ TARGET SKILL

Author's Purpose Tell why an author writes a book.

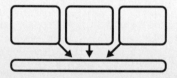

✓ GENRE

Informational text gives facts about a topic. As you read, look for:

- ▸ photos
- ▸ facts and details about a topic
- ▸ headings that begin a section

COMMON CORE **LACC.2.RI.2.6** identify the main purpose of a text; **LACC.2.RI.4.10** read and comprehend informational texts

MEET THE AUTHOR

Jennifer Blizin Gillis

Jennifer Blizin Gillis wrote her first story in the third grade. It was a mystery story that was four pages long! She has now written lots of books. She has written about pets, people, and even ballroom dancing. Besides writing, she likes to read, work in her garden, and cook. She also takes care of some pets of her own. She has two dogs and a cat.

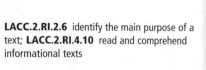

Dogs

by Jennifer Blizin Gillis

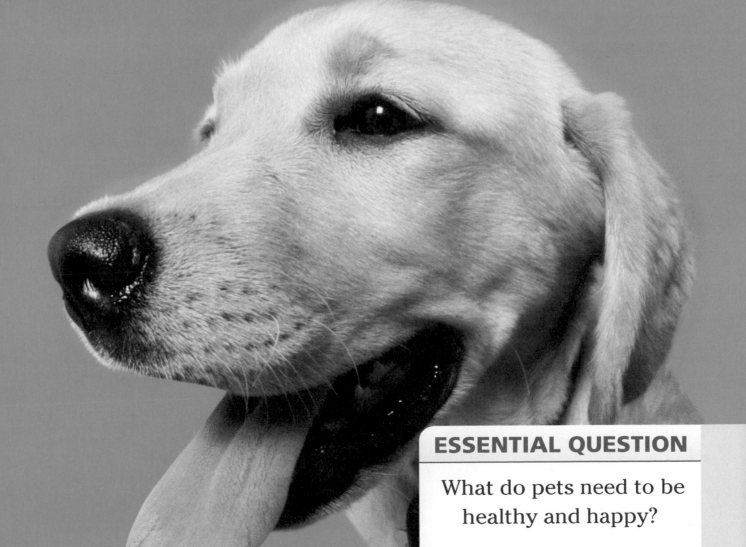

What Kind of Pet Is This?

Pets are animals that live with us. Some pets are small and have feathers. My pet is big and hairy. Can you guess what kind of pet this is?

What Are Dogs?

Dogs are mammals. Mammals make milk for their babies. Dogs are cousins of wolves and coyotes. Most dogs live with people as pets.

Where Did My Dog Come From?

A mother dog had a litter of puppies. At first, the puppies could not see. The puppies stayed with their mother for eight weeks. Then I took a puppy home.

How Big Is My Dog?

At first, my dog was as small as a cat. It weighed as much as a big bag of sugar. Now my puppy is a dog. It weighs as much as a bicycle.

Where Does My Dog Live?

My dog lives in the house with us. It sleeps on a special dog bed. Sometimes my dog sleeps in my room. It may even sleep on my bed.

What Does My Dog Eat?

My dog eats canned dog food. Sometimes my dog eats dry dog food. My dog chews special bones, too. Chewing the bones helps keep its teeth strong and clean.

What Else Does My Dog Need?

My dog needs a collar and a nametag. These can help me find it if it gets lost. My dog needs a leash, too. The leash is clipped to the collar so my dog can go for a walk.

ANALYZE THE TEXT

Author's Purpose What question does the author want to answer on this page?

What Can I Do For My Dog?

I play with my dog every day. Playing is good exercise for dogs. I brush my dog with a special brush. This keeps its coat clean and smooth.

What Can My Dog Do?

My dog can play fetch. When I throw a ball, it brings it back. My dog can help at home. It can bring in the newspaper.

Dig Deeper

How to Analyze the Text

Use these pages to learn about Author's Purpose and Compare and Contrast. Then read *Dogs* again. Use what you learn to understand it better.

Author's Purpose

Dogs is about how to care for a pet dog. The author wrote this selection for a reason. The reason an author writes is the **author's purpose.** The author may write to help you learn about something or to make you smile.

As you read, think about why the author wrote *Dogs*. Use a chart like the one below to list text evidence. Use the evidence to help you figure out what the author wants you to know.

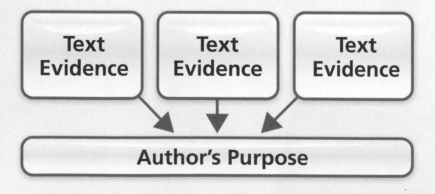

Text Evidence	Text Evidence	Text Evidence

Author's Purpose

LACC.2.RI.1.3 describe the connection between a series of historical events/scientific ideas/steps in technical procedures; **LACC.2.RI.2.6** identify the main purpose of a text

Compare and Contrast

Sometimes an author tells how things are the same and different. For example, an author may tell how two animals are the same and different. Telling how things are the same is called **comparing.** Telling how things are different is called **contrasting.** As you read, compare and contrast to help you understand ideas from the text.

Your Turn

What do pets need to be healthy and happy?
Think about what you read in *Dogs*. Then talk with a partner about your ideas. Use text evidence to explain your thoughts. Ask questions if you do not understand what your partner says.

Classroom Conversation

Now talk about these questions with the class.

1 What does the author want you to learn about dogs? Give text evidence to explain.

2 How do people take care of their dogs?

3 Why do people have dogs as pets?

Response Would you like to care for a dog as a pet? Write a few sentences to tell your opinion. Use evidence from the text to help you explain.

Writing Tip

In the first sentence, tell if you would or would not like a dog. Tell your reasons in the other sentences.

Helping Paws

☑ **GENRE**

Informational Text gives facts about a topic.

☑ **TEXT FOCUS**

Captions tell more information about photos.

Helping Paws

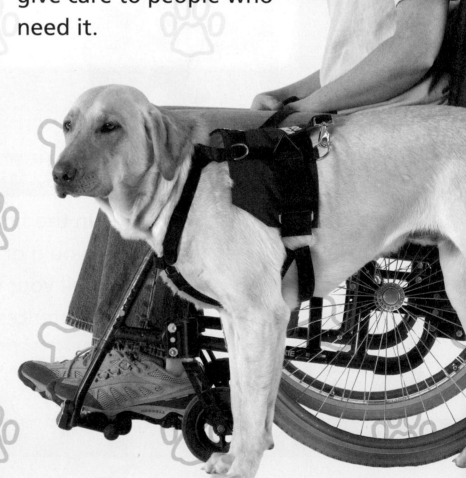

Most people think of dogs as pets. For many people, dogs are family helpers! Some dogs help people who have disabilities. They give care to people who need it.

COMMON CORE **LACC.2.RI.2.5** know and use text features to locate facts or information; **LACC.2.RI.4.10** read and comprehend informational texts

Hearing Ear Dogs

Hearing ear dogs help people who are deaf or who cannot hear well. These dogs listen for important sounds at home. An alarm clock and a doorbell are important sounds. When the dogs hear these sounds, they touch their owners with their noses. This gets their owners' attention. When hearing ear dogs are outside with their owners, they listen for sounds that could mean danger. They help keep their owners safe.

Hearing Ear Dogs Are Helpers

- They listen for important sounds inside and outside.

- They let their owners know if there is danger.

Hearing ear dogs listen for the ring of a telephone or the sound of a smoke detector.

Guide Dogs Are Helpers

- Guide dogs help their owners walk safely.

- They follow directions to help their owners.

Guide Dogs

Guide dogs help people who are blind or cannot see well. A guide dog learns sights, sounds, and smells of busy places. Guide dogs can go anywhere their owners need to go. They follow directions from their owners.

Make sure not to pet a guide dog when it is working.

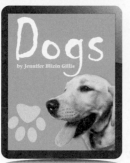 

Compare Texts

TEXT TO TEXT

Write a Paragraph How would page 81 of *Dogs* be written if the selection were about Mudge? With a partner, rewrite the paragraph to be about Mudge.

TEXT TO SELF

Share Experiences Think about the dogs in *Helping Paws*. How do the pets that live with you or near you help people? Share your ideas with a partner.

TEXT TO WORLD

Share Ideas What else can pets do to help their owners? Write a few sentences to tell your ideas.

COMMON CORE **LACC.2.W.1.2** write informative/explanatory texts; **LACC.2.W.1.3** write narratives; **LACC.2.SL.2.4** tell a story or recount an experience with facts and details, speaking audibly in sentences

Grammar

Kinds of Sentences A **statement** tells something. A **command** gives an order. They each end with a period. An **exclamation** shows strong feeling. It ends with an exclamation point. A **question** asks something. It ends with a question mark.

Statement	Some dogs can be trained to help people.
Question	Can a dog help a person who is deaf?
Command	Do not pet a working guide dog.
Exclamation	She is a great guide dog!

Try This! **Decide whether each sentence is a statement, a command, an exclamation, or a question. Write each sentence with the correct end mark.**

1. What did the dog hear

2. Be careful when you cross a street

3. Guide dogs help keep their owners safe

4. His guide dog is so helpful

Using different kinds of sentences makes your writing more interesting to read. You can change one kind of sentence to another by moving or adding words.

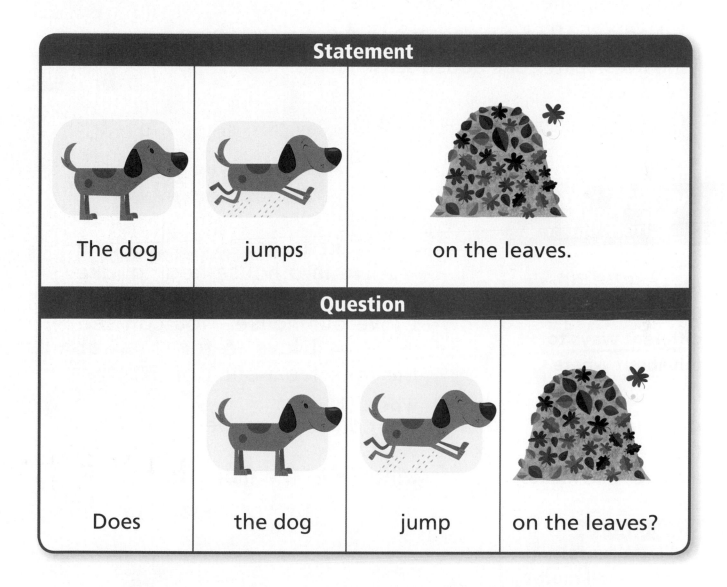

Statement		
The dog	jumps	on the leaves.

Question			
Does	the dog	jump	on the leaves?

🖊 Connect Grammar to Writing

When you revise your writing, try using different kinds of sentences to make your writing more interesting.

Narrative Writing

You can make a **description** more interesting when you use sense words to tell how things look, feel, smell, sound, and taste.

Nadia drafted a paragraph that describes where she lives. Later, she added sense words.

Writing Traits Checklist

✔ **Ideas**
Did I think of different ways to tell about where I live?

✔ **Organization**
Did I tell things in an order that makes sense?

✔ **Word Choice**
Did I use sense words to tell more?

✔ **Sentence Fluency**
Did I use different kinds of sentences?

Revised Draft

little green   big blue
I live in a house near a lake.
          ∧   ∧

I love our house. You can see
          I love to feel the warm
the lake from our porch. ~~The~~
                          ∧
when it
sun ∧comes in my bedroom

window in the morning.

My House
by Nadia Krimsky

I live in a little green house near a big blue lake. I love our house. You can see the lake from our porch. I love to feel the warm sun when it comes in my bedroom window in the morning. Do you know what wakes me up? The birds start chirping. I smell the pancakes my dad makes. They taste so good that I always ask for more! I want to live in this house for a long time.

Reading as a Writer

Which sense words did Nadia add? What sense words can you add to your writing?

I used sense words to tell the reader more about how things look, feel, smell, taste, and sound.

By Doreen Cronin · Pictures by Harry Bliss

DIARY OF A SPIDER

A SWALLOW AND A SPIDER

☑ **TARGET VOCABULARY**

insects

dangerous

scare

sticky

rotten

screaming

breeze

judge

Vocabulary Reader

Along Came a SPIDER...

Context Cards

COMMON CORE

LACC.2.L.3.6 use words and phrases acquired through conversations, reading and being read to, and responding to texts

Go Digital

102

Vocabulary in Context

▶ **Read each Context Card.**

▶ **Ask a question that uses one of the Vocabulary words.**

1 **insects**

Ants, flies, and bees are all insects. They all have six legs.

2 **dangerous**

Be careful! A bee sting can be dangerous. It makes some people sick.

3 **scare**

Cockroaches will run away if you scare them. They frighten easily.

4 **sticky**

A spider web is sticky. Bugs get caught, and they can't fly away.

5 **rotten**

A housefly eats rotten, or spoiled, food.

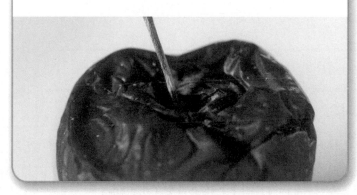

6 **screaming**

If you see a wasp, walk away quietly. Don't run away screaming.

7 **breeze**

A ladybug came in when a breeze blew open the window curtains.

8 **judge**

Look carefully before you judge, or decide, what this picture shows.

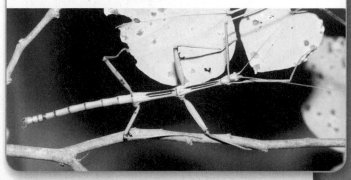

103

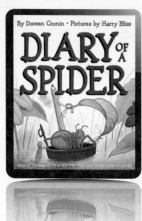

Read and Comprehend

☑ **TARGET SKILL**

Cause and Effect Some people see a spider and get scared. The two events are linked. Seeing the spider is the **cause**. Becoming scared is the **effect**.

Look at the words and pictures in a story to figure out what happens and why. You can use a chart like the one below to list causes and effects.

Cause	Effect

☑ **TARGET STRATEGY**

Summarize Stop to tell important events as you read.

LACC.2.RL.3.7 use information from illustrations and words to demonstrate understanding of characters, setting, or plot

104

Getting Along with Others

Diary of a Spider is a made-up story about a spider who is friends with a fly. Think about why it might be hard for a spider and a fly to be friends. For one thing, a fly spends a lot of time in the air, but a spider can't fly. Also, a fly might get caught in a spider's web. Spider and Fly have fun together even though they are different. They learn to work around their differences to get along together.

ANCHOR TEXT

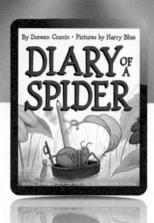

By Doreen Cronin • Pictures by Harry Bliss

DIARY OF A SPIDER

✓ TARGET SKILL

Cause and Effect Tell how one event makes another happen.

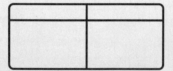

✓ GENRE

Humorous fiction is a story that is written to make the reader laugh. As you read, look for:

► characters who do or say funny things
► events that would not happen in real life

 COMMON CORE **LACC.2.RL.2.4** describe how words and phrases supply rhythm and meaning; **LACC.2.RL.3.7** use information from illustrations and words to demonstrate understanding of characters, setting, or plot; **LACC.2.RL.4.10** read and comprehend literature

MEET THE AUTHOR

Doreen Cronin

Two spiders have moved into Doreen Cronin's office, but she says she cannot bring herself to get rid of them. If you like *Diary of a Spider*, check out Ms. Cronin's other books, *Diary of a Worm* and *Diary of a Fly*.

MEET THE ILLUSTRATOR

Harry Bliss

Whenever Harry Bliss visits classrooms, he asks students to scribble on the board. He then turns their scribbles into an animal, a tree, or a cartoon character. This scribble game helps kids use their imagination.

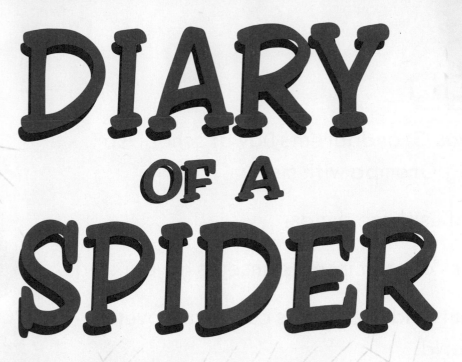

DIARY
OF A
SPIDER

by **Doreen Cronin**
pictures by **Harry Bliss**

MARCH 1

Today was Grandparents Day at school, so
I brought Grampa with me.

He taught us three things:

1. Spiders are not insects—insects have six legs.

2. Without spiders, insects could take over
   the world.

3. Butterflies taste better with a little
   barbecue sauce.

MARCH 16

Grampa says that in his day, flies and spiders did not get along.

Things are different now.

MARCH 29

Today in gym class we learned how to catch the wind so we could travel to faraway places.

When I got home, I made up flash cards so I could practice:

Fly made up her own flash card:

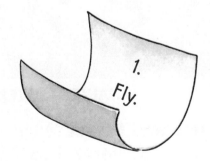

I'm starting to see why Grampa doesn't like her.

APRIL 1

I went to the park with my sister today. We tried the seesaw.

It didn't work.

ANALYZE THE TEXT

Cause and Effect Why does the seesaw not work? Use the illustration to help you.

We tried the tire swing.

It didn't work.

We spun a huge sticky web on the water fountain.

That worked.

EEEEEEK!

113

APRIL 12

Today was Safety Day at school. We learned that vacuums eat spiderwebs and are very, very dangerous. If we hear a vacuum, we should Stop, Drop, and Run.

STOP WHAT WE'RE DOING. DROP FROM THE WEB. RUN LIKE CRAZY.

PARTY CANDLES 40 CT.

CANDLES

APRIL 13

We had a vacuum drill today.
I stopped what I was doing.

Forgot where I was going.

And ran screaming from the room.

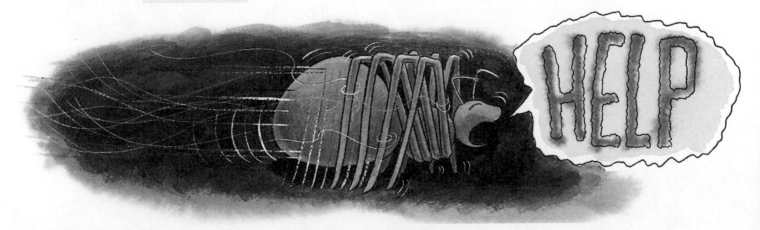

We're having another drill tomorrow.

APRIL 17

I'm sleeping over at Worm's house tonight. I hope they don't have leaves and rotten tomatoes for dinner again.

MAY 7

Mom said I was getting too big for my own skin. So I molted.

MAY 8

Today was show-and-tell. So I brought in my old skin. My teacher called on it to lead the Pledge of Allegiance.

JUNE 5

Daddy Longlegs made fun of Fly because she eats with her feet. Now she won't come out of her tree house.

I'm going to find him and give him a piece of my mind!

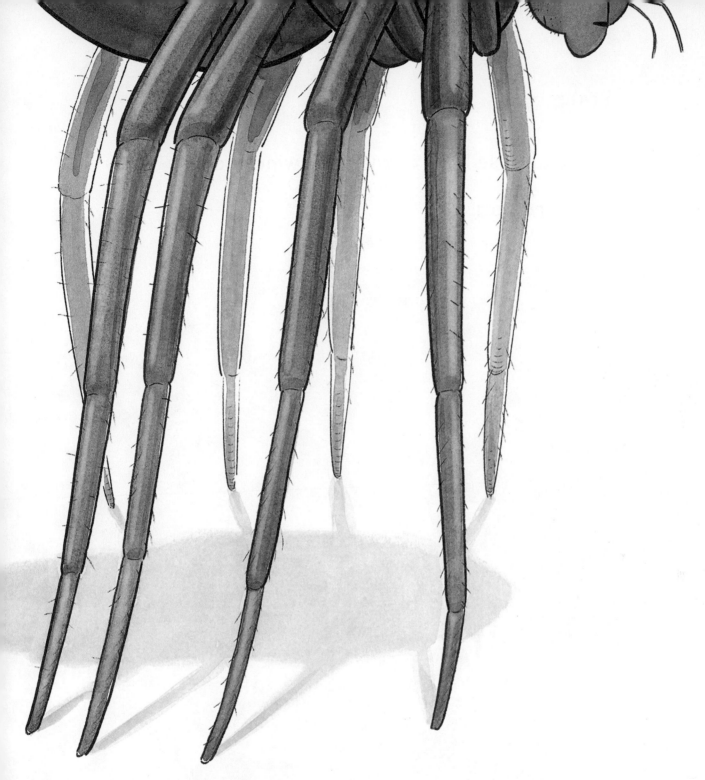

JUNE 6

I found Daddy Longlegs. He's a lot bigger than
I thought he was.

I gave him a piece of my lunch instead.

JUNE 7

Fly's tree house blew away in the wind today.

So did Grampa.

JUNE 18

I got a postcard from Grampa today:

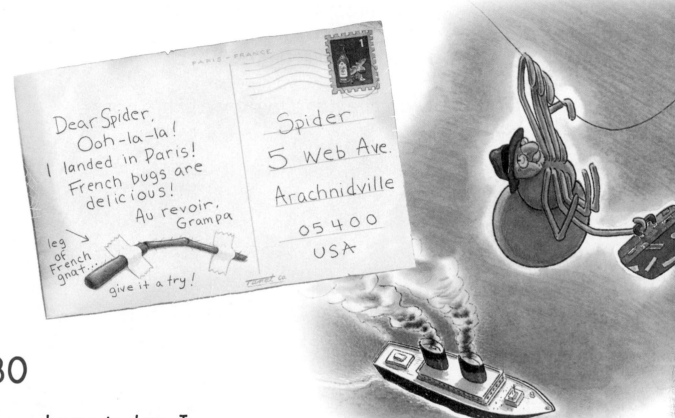

Dear Spider,
Ooh-la-la!
I landed in Paris!
French bugs are delicious!
Au revoir,
Grampa

leg of French gnat... give it a try!

PARIS - FRANCE

Spider
5 Web Ave.
Arachnidville
05400
USA

JUNE 30

Grampa came home today. I couldn't wait to hear about how he rode the winds all the way over the ocean!

Turns out, he caught a breeze to the airport and napped in first class.

ANALYZE THE TEXT

Personification What does Grampa do that makes him seem like a person? Use the words and the pictures to help you answer.

JULY 2

Fly came over to play today. She got stuck in our web, and her mom had to come get her.

Grampa laughed a little too hard.

From now on, we have to play at Fly's house.

JULY 9

Today was my birthday. Grampa decided I was old enough to know the secret to a long, happy life:

Never fall asleep in a shoe.

JULY 16

Things I scare:

1. Fly's mom

It wasn't his fault, Mom.

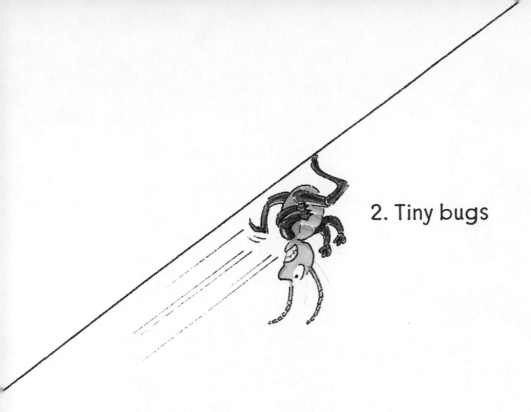

2. Tiny bugs

3. People using water
fountains at the park

JULY 17

Things that scare me:

1. Daddy Longlegs

2. Vacuums

3. People with big feet

127

AUGUST 1

I wish that people wouldn't judge all spiders based on the few spiders that bite.

I know if we took the time to get to know each other, we would get along just fine.

Just like me and Fly.

SPIDER'S CLUBHOUSE

Dig Deeper

How to Analyze the Text

Use these pages to learn about Cause and Effect and Personification. Then read *Diary of a Spider* again. Use what you learn to understand it better.

Cause and Effect

Diary of a Spider is a funny story about Spider and his friend, Fly. In the story, one event makes another happen. For example, Spider gets too big for his skin, so he sheds it. Spider getting too big is the **cause**. Spider shedding his skin is the **effect**.

When you read, ask questions about the words and pictures to figure out what happens and why. Use a chart to list text evidence of causes and effects.

Cause	Effect

LACC.2.RL.2.4 describe how words and phrases supply rhythm and meaning; **LACC.2.RL.3.7** use information from illustrations and words to demonstrate understanding of characters, setting, or plot

130

Personification

Sometimes an author will make animals or objects in a story act or speak like people. For example, an animal might wear clothing that a person would wear. This is called **personification**. Look back at page 111. Spider makes flash cards to help him study. Since spiders don't write, this is an example of personification.

Your Turn

RETURN TO THE ESSENTIAL QUESTION

 How do good friends act?
Find text evidence from the words and pictures in the story. Talk about your ideas with a small group. Let everyone take a turn speaking.

Classroom Conversation

Now talk about these questions with the class.

1 What events in the story cause other events to happen?

2 What problems do Spider and Fly work around in order to be friends?

3 What are some important lessons that Spider learns? Explain your answer with text evidence.

WRITE ABOUT READING

Response By the end of the story, Spider has learned many important things. Write about one important lesson that Spider learns. Give text evidence to tell why you think it is important.

Writing Tip

Use the word *because* to link your reasons to your opinion.

COMMON CORE **LACC.2.RL.3.7** use information from illustrations and words to demonstrate understanding of characters, setting, or plot; **LACC.2.W.1.1** write opinion pieces; **LACC.2.SL.1.1.a** follow rules for discussions

☑ GENRE

A **fable** is a short story in which a character learns a lesson.

☑ TEXT FOCUS

The **moral** of a fable is the lesson that a character learns. As you read, find the moral of the story.

COMMON CORE LACC.2.RL.1.2 recount stories and determine their message, lesson, or moral; **LACC.2.RL.4.10** read and comprehend literature

Readers' Theater

A SWALLOW AND A SPIDER

A FABLE FROM AESOP

retold by Sheila Higginson

Cast of Characters

Narrator   **Spider**   **Swallow**

~~~~~~~~~~~~~~~~~~~~~~~~~

Narrator: A spider sat in her sticky web, waiting for dinner.

Spider: I hope some insects will stop by soon.

Narrator: Spider heard the buzz of flies floating in the breeze.

Swallow: Look at those juicy flies!

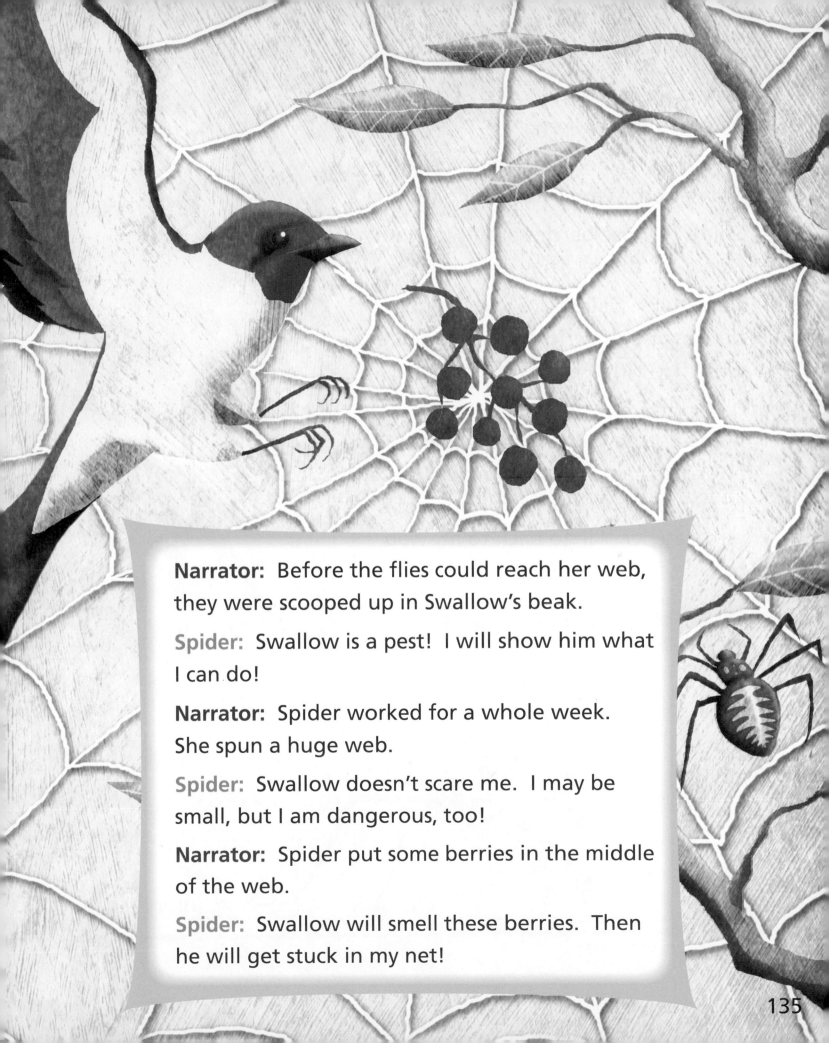

Narrator: Before the flies could reach her web, they were scooped up in Swallow's beak.

Spider: Swallow is a pest! I will show him what I can do!

Narrator: Spider worked for a whole week. She spun a huge web.

Spider: Swallow doesn't scare me. I may be small, but I am dangerous, too!

Narrator: Spider put some berries in the middle of the web.

Spider: Swallow will smell these berries. Then he will get stuck in my net!

135

Narrator: Spider watched and waited, waited and watched.

Swallow: I smell something delicious. Those berries are just waiting for me!

Spider: Those berries aren't for you! Don't eat them! They are rotten.

Narrator: Swallow scooped up the berries and flew right through spider's web! He didn't even hear spider screaming at him!

Spider: I can judge what I am good at doing. I am good at building webs to catch insects, but I am not a good bird-catcher. I'll go back to my web to wait for a juicy fly.

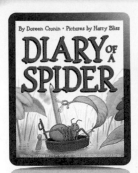

Compare Texts

Compare and Contrast Spider and Fly in *Diary of a Spider* are friends. How is this different from how the characters feel about each other in *A Swallow and a Spider*? Share your thoughts with a partner.

Think About the Moral Think about the moral in *A Swallow and a Spider*. Does this moral apply to your life? Why or why not? Discuss your thoughts and feelings about it with a partner.

Connect to Science Make a poster to teach your classmates about real spiders. Talk with a partner about what the spiders are like in *Diary of a Spider* and *A Swallow and a Spider*. Use the stories or science books to help you.

COMMON CORE **LACC.2.RL.1.2** recount stories and determine their message, lesson, or moral

Grammar

What Is a Noun? A **noun** is a word that names a person, an animal, a place, or a thing.

People	Animals
grandfather	spider
girl	fly
friend	bird
Places	**Things**
home	web
school	vacuum
park	tomato

Try This! **Work with a partner. Find the noun in each sentence. Tell whether it is a person, an animal, a place, or a thing.**

1. Our swing did not move.

2. The worm sleeps.

3. My teacher is nice.

4. The airport is big.

When you write, use exact nouns to paint a picture in your reader's mind. An exact noun gives more information about a person, an animal, a place, or a thing.

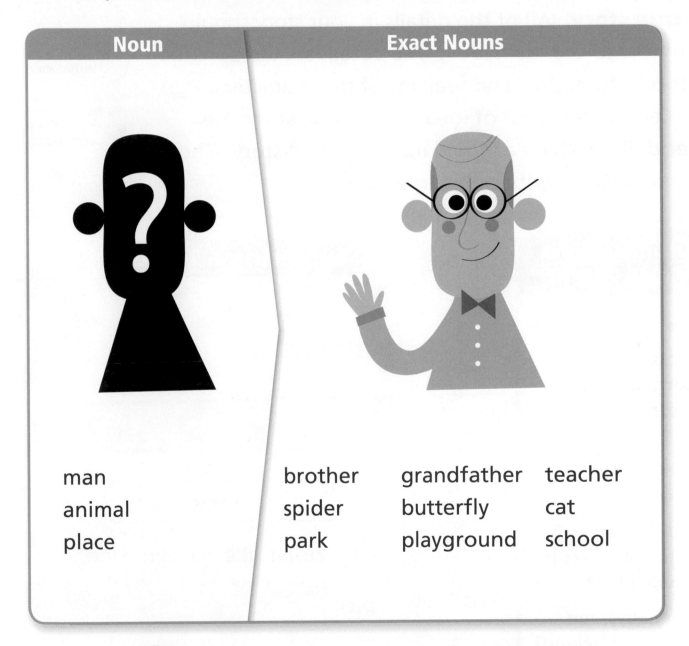

Noun	Exact Nouns		
man	brother	grandfather	teacher
animal	spider	butterfly	cat
place	park	playground	school

 ## Connect Grammar to Writing

As you revise your true story next week, look for nouns you could replace with exact nouns.

Reading-Writing Workshop: Prewrite

Narrative Writing

✓ **Ideas** The main idea is the most important part of a **true story.** All of the details in your story should connect to the main idea. The details should describe actions, thoughts, and feelings of the characters.

Kevin made a list of ideas for his true story. He decided which idea would make the best story. Then he made an idea web for his true story.

Writing Process Checklist

▶ **Prewrite**

☑ **What is the most important idea of my story?**

☑ **What details tell about what happened?**

☑ **Do all the parts of the story connect to the main idea?**

☑ **Is there anything that doesn't belong?**

Draft

Revise

Edit

Publish and Share

Exploring a Topic

basketball

my sister's cat

video games

(me in the author's chair)

why I don't like to practice

piano

Idea Web

reading my story about Uncle Li and the spider

nervous about reading my story

My Turn in the Author's Chair

practicing in front of my family

class claps for my story

Reading as a Writer

How do Kevin's details in the outer circles connect with the main idea? Which details will you use to connect with your main idea?

I added details to the web that connect to the main idea.

Teacher's Pets

Dayle Ann Dodds Illustrated by Marylin Hafner

See Westburg
by Bus!

BUS

☑ **TARGET VOCABULARY**

wonderful

noises

quiet

sprinkled

share

noticed

bursting

suddenly

Vocabulary
Reader

Context
Cards

Fun
Pets

wonderful
Pets are wonderful. They
make very good friends.

Wonderful

COMMON
CORE

LACC.2.L.3.6 use words and phrases acquired
through conversations, reading and being read to,
and responding to texts

Go
Digital

Vocabulary
in Context

▶ Read each Context Card.

▶ Tell a story about two
pictures using the
Vocabulary words.

1   **wonderful**

Pets are wonderful. They
make very good friends.

2   **noises**

Big dogs bark loudly. Small
dogs do not make such loud
noises.

3 quiet

A lizard is a very quiet pet. It does not make a sound.

4 sprinkled

The fish food was lightly sprinkled on top of the water.

5 share

Take pictures of your pets to share with your friends.

6 noticed

This pet rabbit noticed, or looked carefully, at the carrot held for it to eat.

7 bursting

Look at this crowded basket. It is bursting with puppies!

8 suddenly

A pet parrot might surprise you if it suddenly says a word.

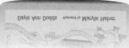

Read and Comprehend

☑ TARGET SKILL

Story Structure The people who are in a story are **characters**. The **setting** of a story is where and when the story takes place. The **plot** is what happens in the story.

As you read *Teacher's Pets,* think about where the story takes place and who is in it. Think about what happens, too. You can use a story map like the one below to tell the main parts of the story.

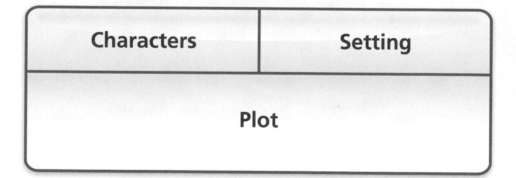

Characters	Setting
Plot	

☑ TARGET STRATEGY

Visualize Picture what is happening as you read.

LACC.2.RL.2.5 describe the overall structure of a story

COMMON CORE

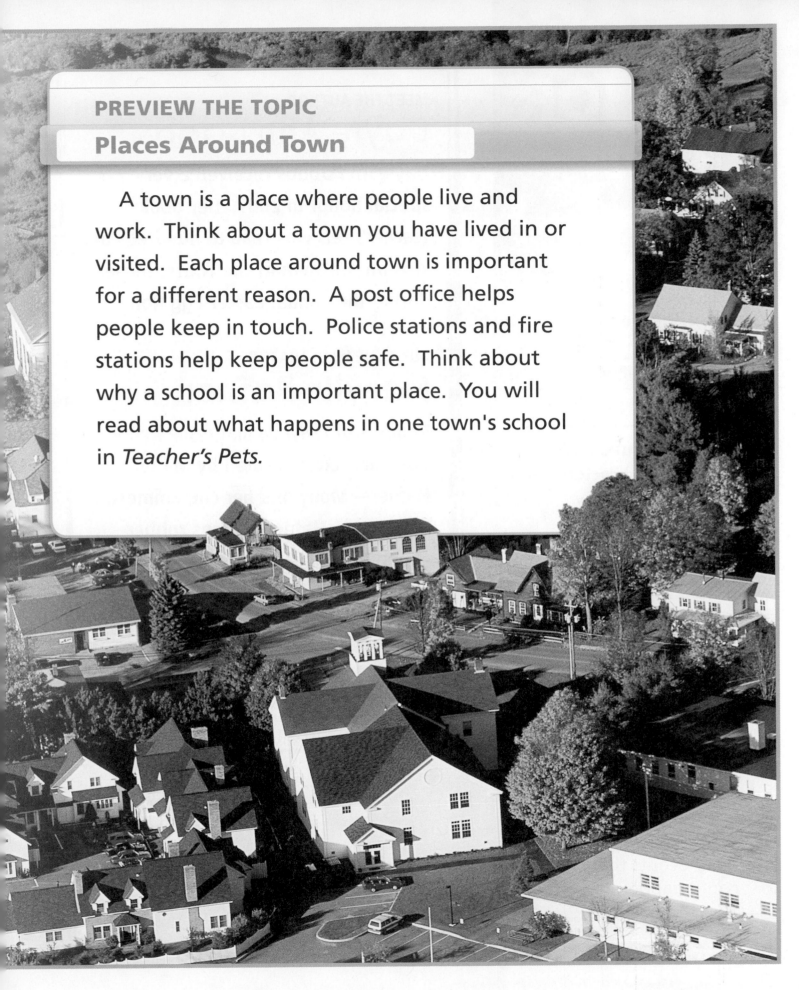

Places Around Town

A town is a place where people live and work. Think about a town you have lived in or visited. Each place around town is important for a different reason. A post office helps people keep in touch. Police stations and fire stations help keep people safe. Think about why a school is an important place. You will read about what happens in one town's school in *Teacher's Pets.*

ANCHOR TEXT

✓ TARGET SKILL

Story Structure Tell the setting, characters, and plot in the story.

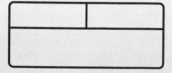

✓ GENRE

Realistic fiction is a story that could really happen. As you read, look for:

► characters who act like real people

► a setting that could be a real place

► story events that could happen to you

COMMON CORE **LACC.2.RL.2.4** describe how words and phrases supply rhythm and meaning; **LACC.2.RL.2.5** describe the overall structure of a story; **LACC.2.RL.4.10** read and comprehend literature

146

MEET THE AUTHOR

Dayle Ann Dodds

Dayle Ann Dodds received a very special honor in 2007. Her book *Teacher's Pets* was read to hundreds of kids on the lawn of the White House during the annual Easter Egg Roll.

MEET THE ILLUSTRATOR

Marylin Hafner

Readers of *Ladybug* magazine know two characters created by Marylin Hafner—Molly and her cat, Emmett. For fun Ms. Hafner designs rubber stamps, usually with kids or animals on them.

Teacher's Pets

by **Dayle Ann Dodds**
illustrated by **Marylin Hafner**

ESSENTIAL QUESTION

How is a school like
a community?

Monday was sharing day in Miss Fry's class.

"You may bring something special," said Miss Fry.

"May we share a pet?" Winston asked.

"Yes," said Miss Fry. "But just for the day."

On Monday, Winston brought in his pet rooster.

"I call him Red. He eats corn, and he crows. The neighbors say he crows too much."

"What a wonderful pet," said Miss Fry. "We're happy he can visit us today."

But that afternoon, after all the children had left, there was Red, still sitting on his roost near Miss Fry's desk.

She sprinkled corn in Red's dish, then locked the
door and went home to her quiet little house.

On Tuesday, Winston told Miss Fry, "The neighbors
wonder if Red can stay at school for a while."

"Of course," said Miss Fry. "How lucky for us."

The next Monday was Patrick's turn. "My tarantula's name is Vincent. He likes to eat bugs and hide inside my mother's slippers."

"What a wonderful pet," said Miss Fry. "Don't forget to take Vincent home with you at the end of the day."

But that afternoon, after all the children had left,
there was Vincent, still sitting in his jar on Miss Fry's
desk. She gave Vincent a big juicy bug, sprinkled corn
on Red's dish, then locked the door and went home to
her quiet little house.

On Tuesday, Patrick told Miss Fry, "My mother says Vincent likes her slippers too much. We're wondering if he can stay at school for a few days."

"Of course," said Miss Fry. "How lucky for us."

The next week, Roger brought in his cricket.

"His name is Moe," said Roger. "He eats leaves from the garden and sings *chirrup-chirrup* all night long."

"What a wonderful pet," said Miss Fry.

ANALYZE THE TEXT

Author's Word Choice What does Miss Fry say every time a child asks if a pet can stay? What does this tell you about Miss Fry?

That afternoon, after all the children had left, Miss Fry noticed Moe sitting in his box on the table. Miss Fry looked at Moe. He almost seemed to smile. "Welcome to our class, Moe."

Right before her eyes, he did a huge somersault—up, up in the air. "Bravo!" said Miss Fry.

She gave fresh green leaves to Moe and a big juicy bug to Vincent, sprinkled corn in Red's dish, then locked the door and went home to her quiet little house.

The next day, Roger said to Miss Fry, "My mother says Moe chirps too much."

"He's welcome to visit as long as he likes," said Miss Fry.

And so it went.

Alia shared her pet goat named Gladys. It said *Baaaaa!* and ate her sister's homework.

Amanda shared her pet dachshund. It liked to chew bones and the pillows on her aunt Judy's new sofa.

Jerry brought in his pet boa constrictor. It never made a sound. No one knew exactly what it liked to eat, but Jerry said his father's expensive tropical fish had suddenly disappeared one day.

There was Megan's cat,

Mitchell's mice,

Daniel's ducks,

and Tom's iguana.

Frankie's frog,

Lily's monkey,

Terrence's turtle . . .

159

and something square and fuzzy that Avery brought in.

"It looks like a kitchen sponge," said Bruce. "A *really old* kitchen sponge."

"It's my pet," said Avery, and that was that.

Before long, Miss Fry's classroom was bursting
with the happy noises of all the children's pets.

On Parents' Night, the mothers and fathers walked around
the classroom with great big smiles on their faces.
"Isn't it great," they said, "that Miss Fry loves pets so?"

Only Roger's cricket sat quietly in his box.

"You must miss your garden," Miss Fry said.

Chirrup, said Moe softly. He crawled under one of his shiny green leaves.

chirrup

On the last day of school, Miss Fry's class had
a party with balloons, hats, and ice-cream cups.
"Good-bye, children!" Miss Fry sang out.
"Have a nice summer . . . *and don't forget to*

take
home
your
pets!"

One by one, the children disappeared,

and with them went their pets.

"No more pets," said Miss Fry.

She looked around the quiet, empty room.

Then Miss Fry noticed a box sitting on her desk.

She peeked inside. A little face looked up at her.

It almost seemed to smile.

A note inside read:

DEAR MISS FRY,
PLEASE TAKE
CARE
OF MOE.
HE LIKES YOU
BEST.

ROGER

"How lucky for me," said Miss Fry.

Moe did a huge somersault—up, up in the air.

Miss Fry carried her new pet to her quiet little house and placed him in the garden, among the rainbow of roses.

That night, Miss Fry opened her window.

She climbed into bed. She turned off the lamp.

By the light of the moon, from outside in the garden, came a happy noise.

Chirrup-chirrup!

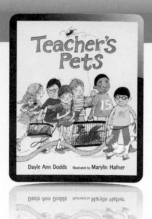

Dig Deeper

How to Analyze the Text

Use these pages to learn about Story Structure and Author's Word Choice. Then read *Teacher's Pets* again. Use what you learn to understand it better.

Story Structure

Teacher's Pets is about what happens when Miss Fry lets everyone bring a pet to class. Who are the characters? Where does the story take place?

Think about how the beginning of the story tells the main story problem. Then think about how the problem is solved in the end. A story map can help you describe the **characters**, **setting**, and **plot**.

Characters	Setting
Plot	

LACC.2.RL.2.4 describe how words and phrases supply rhythm and meaning; **LACC.2.RL.2.5** describe the overall structure of a story

Author's Word Choice

Sometimes an author repeats words, phrases, or events. This is called **repetition**. Repetition makes a story fun to read and easy to remember.

In *Teacher's Pets*, there is a repeating event. Children keep bringing pets into class. The author also repeats words and phrases. Think about how repeated words and phrases in the story help you understand what happens.

Your Turn

RETURN TO THE ESSENTIAL QUESTION

 How is a school like a community? Discuss your ideas with a partner. Use text evidence from *Teacher's Pets* to explain. Ask a question if you don't understand your partner's ideas.

Classroom Conversation

Now talk about these questions with the class.

1. What happens at the beginning of the story that gives you a clue about how it will end?

2. Why does Miss Fry let the students keep their pets at school? How do you know?

3. What type of teacher do you think Miss Fry is? Use text evidence from the story to help you.

Response Reread pages 166–167. Why does Miss Fry say that she is lucky after reading Roger's note? Write a few sentences to tell your opinion. Use text evidence from the words and pictures to give reasons for your answer.

Writing Tip

Make sure that each of your sentences has a subject and a predicate.

COMMON CORE **LACC.2.RL.2.5** describe the overall structure of a story; **LACC.2.RL.3.7** use information from illustrations and words to demonstrate understanding of characters, setting, or plot; **LACC.2.W.1.1** write opinion pieces; **LACC.2.SL.1.1.c** ask for clarification and explanation about topics and texts under discussion

INFORMATIONAL TEXT

☑ GENRE

Informational text gives facts about a topic. This is a pamphlet.

☑ TEXT FOCUS

A **map** is a drawing of a town, state, or other place.

LACC.2.RI.4.10 read and comprehend informational texts

See Westburg by Bus!

BUS

Welcome to Westburg!

The best way to see our town is on Bus Number 33. Get the bus in front of our Welcome Center. After you get on board, read this pamphlet. Just follow the numbers sprinkled on the map as you go.

We are happy to share our wonderful town with you.

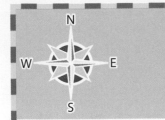

SILVER RIVER

Brown Street

Red Street

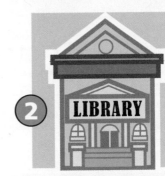

2 LIBRARY

Blue Avenue

1 WELCOME CENTER

Pine Street

3

Rainbow Park

---

1 Welcome Center

Find the Welcome Center. It is bursting with pamphlets, maps, and books about Westburg.

2 Library

The Public Library is on Blue Avenue. The children's room is a great place for books, computer games, and movies.

3 Rainbow Park

Cross Blue Avenue to get to Westburg's largest park. People come here to play, walk, or have some quiet time.

Key

river   bus route ▪ ▪ ▪ ▪   bridge

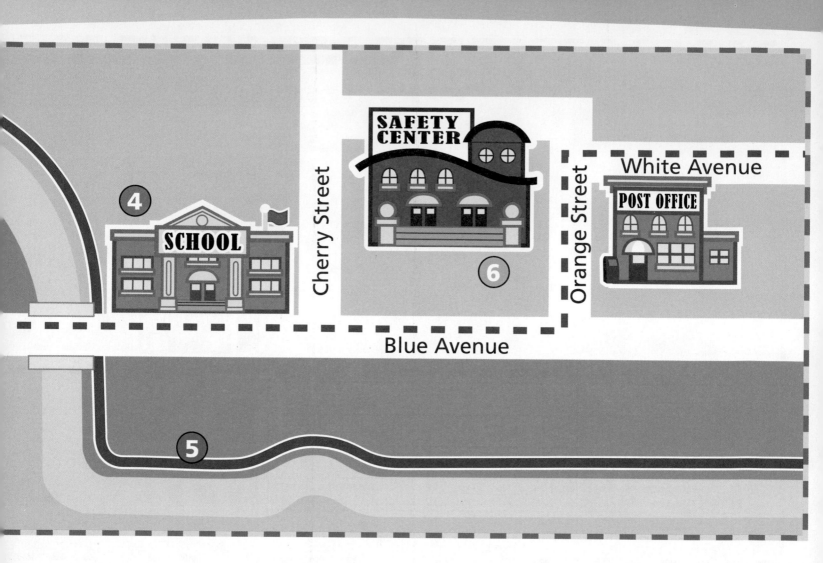

4 School

Take the bridge across the Silver River. When you get on the other side, Cherry Elementary will be on your left.

5 Bike Path

Have you noticed how the bike path follows the curves of the Silver River? What a great view!

6 Safety Center

If you suddenly hear siren noises as you pass the Safety Center, a fire truck or ambulance may be whizzing by!

Compare Texts

TEXT TO TEXT

Make Decisions Discuss Miss Fry's classroom and the town of Westburg with a partner. Which place would you rather live if you were a pet? Why? Use the words and illustrations in each selection to help you answer. Speak in complete sentences.

TEXT TO SELF

Write About School If you were a student in Miss Fry's class, what pet would you bring to school? Why? Write to explain your answer. Share your ideas with a partner.

TEXT TO WORLD

Research an Animal Choose a pet from *Teacher's Pets* that you would like to know more about. Research how to care for that type of pet.

COMMON CORE **LACC.2.RL.3.7** use information from illustrations and words to demonstrate understanding of characters, setting, or plot; **LACC.2.SL.2.6** produce complete sentences to provide detail or clarification

Grammar

Singular and Plural Nouns A **singular noun** names one person, animal, place, or thing. A **plural noun** names more than one person, animal, place, or thing. Add -*s* to most nouns to name more than one.

Sentences with Singular Nouns	Sentences with Plural Nouns
The teacher talks loudly.	The two teachers talk to their students.
This playground looks big.	All playgrounds are fun.

Try This! **Work with a partner. Read the sentences aloud. Name the singular nouns and plural nouns.**

❶ Two crickets sat in a cage.

❷ My friend has three cats.

❸ Her bird ate some seeds.

❹ Our teacher loves pets!

Edit your writing carefully. Make sure you have used the correct plural form for each noun that names more than one.

Singular Nouns	Plural Nouns
one frog	two frogs
a bug	many bugs

 ## Connect Grammar to Writing

When you edit your true story, be sure to write the correct form of all plural nouns.

Reading-Writing Workshop: Revise

Narrative Writing

☑ **Sentence Fluency** When you write a **true story**, use time-order words and details that describe thoughts, feelings, and actions of the characters.

Kevin drafted a story about the day he read a story to the class. Later, he added details to tell when things happened and how he felt.

Writing Process Checklist

Prewrite

Draft

▶ **Revise**

☑ Does my story have a beginning, middle, and end?

☑ Does the beginning make the reader want to read more?

☑ Did I use time-order words to tell when things happened?

☑ Did I add details?

☑ Does the ending wrap things up?

Edit

Publish and Share

Revised Draft

Last week, it
~~It~~ was my turn for the Author's
      ∧
Chair. I chose my story about
                    At first,
Uncle Li and the spider. I was
                         ∧
I thought no one would like my story.
Then,
  nervous. I practiced in front of
          ∧
            I felt ready!
  my family.
            ∧

180

My Day in the Author's Chair
by Kevin Chen

Last week, it was my turn for the Author's Chair. I chose my story about Uncle Li and the spider. At first, I was nervous. I thought no one would like my story. Then, I practiced in front of my family. I felt ready! Finally, I read the story in class. I read the part about how Uncle Li screamed. The class laughed. I was a big hit!

Reading as a Writer

What time-order words does Kevin use? What details can you add to your story?

I used details to tell about thoughts, feelings, and actions.

Read "A Birthday Surprise" and "The King's Woods." As you read, stop and answer each question using text evidence.

A Birthday Surprise

Carlos's mom was baking a cake. "It's for Mrs. Lopez's birthday," she said. "She is eighty-one years old today." Carlos liked their neighbor, Mrs. Lopez. She had some trouble seeing, but it never slowed her down. He wanted to do something special for her to help celebrate her birthday.

1 What causes Carlos to want to do something special for Mrs. Lopez?

Then he got an idea. He got a book and went next door. "Surprise, Mrs. Lopez!" he said. "I'm going to read to you!"

"I love to listen to you read," she said as she stepped out onto the porch.

Carlos and Mrs. Lopez sat down, and Carlos began to read. He glanced up to notice that he had made Mrs. Lopez smile. "That made it all worth it," Carlos thought.

2 What do you know about Carlos from reading the story?

  LACC.2.RL.1.1 ask and answer questions to demonstrate understanding of key details; **LACC.2.RL.1.2** recount stories and determine their message, lesson, or moral; **LACC.2.RL.2.5** describe the overall structure of a story; **LACC.2.RL.3.7** use information from illustrations and words to demonstrate understanding of characters, setting, or plot; **LACC.2.RL.4.10** read and comprehend literature

The King's Woods

Long ago, an old man lived deep in the king's woods. He lived there happily, and no one bothered him. One day, the prince rode through the woods on his horse. He saw the old man and shouted, "Get out of the king's woods! You don't belong here!"

The man went to pack his things. He started to leave the woods to find a new home. Then he saw a sad sight. The prince's horse had fallen. The prince was injured. The old man ran to get help.

3 How is the old man different from the prince?

When the prince was better, he called for the old man. The old man quickly came to the castle. "You saved my life," the prince said. "I was not very friendly to you before, and I'm sorry. You may have anything you want, and I will make sure you get it."

The man didn't even have to think about it. "I only want to stay in the woods," he told the prince. The prince agreed to the man's wish and allowed him to stay as long as he pleased. He lived a happy and peaceful life, and no one bothered him again.

4 What events show that the prince is different at the beginning of the story than he is at the end?

Unit 2

Animals Building Homes

Whose Home Is This?

✓ TARGET VOCABULARY

shaped
branches
pond
beaks
deepest
break
hang
winding

Vocabulary Reader

Context Cards

LACC.2.L.3.6 use words and phrases acquired through conversations, reading and being read to, and responding to texts

Vocabulary in Context

▶ Read each **Context Card**.

▶ Use a Vocabulary word to tell about something you did.

1 **shaped**

Have you ever seen a home shaped like this? It is curved like a ball.

2 **branches**

Tree branches high above the ground are a good home for a sloth.

3 pond

Turtles make their home in a pond, or small lake.

4 beaks

These birds use their beaks to build their home.

5 deepest

The deepest part of the ocean is this eel's home.

6 break

This home won't break! It is made of strong rock.

7 hang

These bats hang upside down in their cave.

8 winding

Some animal homes have long, winding tunnels that twist and turn.

Read and Comprehend

Go Digital

☑ **TARGET SKILL**

Text and Graphic Features An author sometimes adds special text and graphic features to a text. Some examples of **graphic features** are photos and charts. Some examples of **text features** are headings and words in bold print. These features help you find information quickly. They also help you know what an author thinks is important.

You can use a chart like this to list features you find and tell how they help you.

Text or Graphic Feature	Page Number	Purpose

☑ **TARGET STRATEGY**

Question Ask questions about what you are reading. Look for text evidence to answer your questions.

Animal Homes

All animals need homes. Most wild animals find or build homes for themselves. For example, a bear might find a cave to use as its home. A bird builds a nest. Animals' homes help keep them safe, warm, and dry.

You will learn more about where animals live in *Animals Building Homes*.

Animals Building Homes

☑ **TARGET SKILL**

Text and Graphic Features Tell how words and photos help you understand new information.

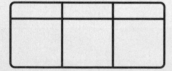

☑ **GENRE**

Informational text gives facts about a topic. As you read, look for:

▸ photos and headings
▸ facts and details about a topic

 COMMON CORE **LACC.2.RI.2.4** determine the meaning of words and phrases in a text; **LACC.2.RI.2.5** know and use text features to locate facts or information; **LACC.2.RI.4.10** read and comprehend informational texts; **LACC.2.L.3.4.a** use sentence-level context as a clue to the meaning of a word or phrase

190

MEET THE AUTHOR

Wendy Perkins

Can you guess why author Wendy Perkins has been called a "walking animal encyclopedia"? It's because her mind is filled with facts and information about all kinds of animals.

Ms. Perkins has written nonfiction books about animal eyes, ears, feet, feathers, noses, teeth, and tails. She also writes articles for *Highlights for Children* and a magazine put out by the San Diego Zoo called *Zoonooz*.

Animals Building Homes

by Wendy Perkins

ESSENTIAL QUESTION

What are animal homes like?

A Beaver's Home

A beaver is hard at work. It gnaws on a tree trunk. Soon, the tree falls. The beaver floats the log to a pond. There, the beaver builds a **lodge**. The beaver piles up logs. It fills the cracks between the logs with mud and grass. The lodge keeps the beaver safe and warm.

ANALYZE THE TEXT

Using Context What is a lodge? How do the other sentences help you to figure out the meaning?

Safe at Home

Most animals need a home. Homes keep animals safe from **predators**, rain, snow, or the hot sun. Some animals live in their homes for life. Other animals live in their homes long enough to raise their **offspring** or **survive** hot or cold weather.

Building Nests

Many animals live in nests. A hummingbird builds a small cup-shaped nest. The nest is made of moss and bits of spiderweb.

A mouse makes a grass nest in the shape of a ball. The mouse hides its nest in tall grass or in a tunnel under the ground.

Careful Builders

Some animals put a lot of work into building their homes. Weaver birds make nests that hang from tree branches. The birds carefully weave grass and leaves together. Weaver birds use their feet and beaks to tie knots in the grass.

Working Together

Animals can work together to build homes. Termites build **mounds** made out of mud mixed with **saliva**. Other animals cannot easily break through the hard mud.

Polyps are animals that make coral reefs. A polyp builds a **limestone** cup around its body for protection. The cups of the polyps grow together to make a coral reef.

Making a Burrow

Burrows are holes in the ground where some animals live. Gophers use their teeth and paws to dig long, winding tunnels. They make rooms in the deepest parts of the tunnels. The gophers hide their offspring and food in these rooms.

ANALYZE THE TEXT

Text and Graphic Features Use the headings to help you quickly find the information about how a gopher makes a burrow. What is the heading for that page?

Home Improvement

Some animals live in homes made by other animals. Chickadees use tree holes made by woodpeckers. Chickadees bring grass and moss into the hole. They build a nest for their chicks.

Building a Home

Most animals need homes where they can rest and raise their offspring. Homes also keep animals safe from predators. Beavers build lodges. Mice make nests. Gophers dig burrows. How does a polar bear make its **den**?

Dig Deeper

How to Analyze the Text

Use these pages to learn about Text and Graphic Features and Using Context. Then read *Animals Building Homes* again. Use what you learn to understand it better.

Text and Graphic Features

The author of *Animals Building Homes* uses text and graphic features to make her ideas clear. For example, the headings help you know what you will read about in each section. They help you find information quickly. Use a chart like this to list text and graphic features and how you use them.

Text or Graphic Feature	Page Number	Purpose

 LACC.2.RI.2.4 determine the meaning of words and phrases in a text; **LACC.2.RI.2.5** know and use text features to locate facts or information; **LACC.2.L.3.4.a** use sentence-level context as a clue to the meaning of a word or phrase

Using Context

Authors sometimes use special words about a topic that may be new to you. You can use other words in the sentence to help figure out what a new word means. Looking at the photos may also help you. Using a sentence or a photo to understand a new word is called **using context**.

Your Turn

What are animal homes like? Share your ideas with a partner. Use the text features and photos from the selection to help you. Point to text evidence to explain your answer to the question.

Classroom Conversation

Now talk about these questions with the class.

1 How can you use the headings to find information in the selection?

2 How are homes that people build the same as and different from the homes that animals build?

3 Why does the author put some words in bold print?

WRITE ABOUT READING

Response Write two facts that you learned about animal homes. Use text evidence such as words and pictures from the selection to help you.

Writing Tip

Remember that a statement tells something. It ends with a period.

✓ GENRE

Informational text gives facts about a topic.

✓ TEXT FOCUS

A **subheading** gives more information about a selection. **Bold print** text shows which words, sentences, or phrases are most important.

COMMON CORE

LACC.2.RI.2.5 know and use text features to locate facts or information; **LACC.2.RI.3.7** explain how images contribute to and clarify text; **LACC.2.RI.3.9** compare and contrast points presented by two texts on the same topic; **LACC.2.RI.4.10** read and comprehend informational texts

Whose Home Is This?

by Joli K. Stevens

Why Do Animals Need Homes?

Animals need homes just like we do to stay safe and warm. Look at the pictures of animal homes on the next few pages. Can you guess what kind of animal might live in each home?

This nest looks like a pile of dead leaves and branches. It is an animal's home!

Many animals make their nests in trees. These nests are made from things the animals can find close by. Things such as leaves, twigs, moss, or feathers are used in nests.

Who lives here?

Some squirrels live in trees.

Squirrels have large, strong claws that help them climb and jump.

Birds are not the only animals that live in tree nests. A large cluster, or bunch, of leaves and twigs high in a tree might be a squirrel's nest. Baby squirrels can stay in the nest for up to ten weeks. A squirrel might use a nest for a few months or even a few years. Sometimes squirrels will build more than one nest and use them all!

These insects are building their home.

There are thousands of small insects that live and work together in this tree. This insect is often called busy because it is always working!

Who lives here?

213

Bees work together in a hive.

A beehive is a very busy place.

A beehive is made up of parts called combs. Bees make the combs out of wax from their own bodies. The cells, or small spaces, near the edge of the comb hold honey. The cells in the middle are where the queen bee lays the eggs. Some bees look after the hive. Other bees collect nectar from flowers to make their food, or honey.

214

There are many kinds of animals that live in or near the ocean. Can you guess what kind of animal might live in a shell?

Who lives here?

An empty shell like this one was once home for an animal.

215

Hermit crabs carry their homes with them.

The hermit crabs along the shore can be very shy around people.

A hermit crab does not have a hard shell. It uses another animal's shell for cover. When an animal gives up its shell, a hermit crab may use it for its own. When a crab grows too large for its shell, it will molt, or cast off the old shell. Then it will get a new one. Would you like to live in a shell?

Compare Texts

Alike and Different Think about the most important ideas about animal homes in each selection. What did you learn from each that is the same? What is different? To answer, look for text evidence with a small group.

Share Experiences Think about the animal homes in *Animals Building Homes*. Which have you seen before? Share your ideas with a partner.

Classify Animals With a small group, sort the animals in each selection by the type of home they build, such as a hole or a nest. Research other animals that live in those types of homes. Make a chart to share with the class.

Go Digital

COMMON CORE **LACC.2.RI.3.9** compare and contrast points presented by two texts on same topic; **LACC.2.W.3.7** participate in shared research and writing projects

Grammar

Special Kinds of Nouns Special nouns that end with *s*, *x*, *ch*, or *sh* get a different ending when they tell about more than one. Add -*es* to these nouns to make them **plural.** Other special nouns change spelling to name more than one. A **collective noun** names a group of things.

Plural Nouns	Collective Nouns
two foxes	the team
many classes	a class
some finches	my family
three dishes	an army
four children	the herd

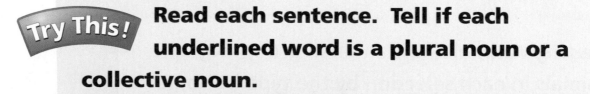

Try This! **Read each sentence. Tell if each underlined word is a plural noun or a collective noun.**

❶ The <u>herd</u> of deer ran away quickly!

❷ The <u>bushes</u> hide animal homes.

❸ The three <u>mice</u> ate the cheese.

❹ Where did the <u>flock</u> go?

When you write, check that all special nouns are spelled correctly when talking about more than one.

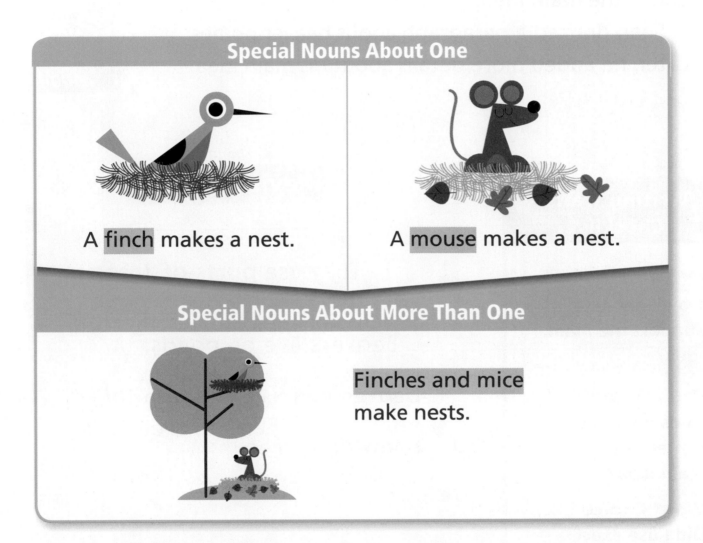

Special Nouns About One

A finch makes a nest.

A mouse makes a nest.

Special Nouns About More Than One

Finches and mice make nests.

 Connect Grammar to Writing

When you revise your writing, find special nouns that tell about more than one. Be sure the nouns follow the rules you have learned.

Informative Writing

✓ **Ideas** When you write an **informational paragraph,** make sure you include details that tell about the main idea.

Sean drafted a paragraph about beaver homes. Later, he added more details about his main idea.

Writing Traits Checklist

 Ideas

Do all my details support the main idea?

✓ **Organization**
Does my topic sentence tell the main idea?

✓ **Word Choice**
Did I use exact words?

✓ **Conventions**
Did I write neatly and leave margins?

Revised Draft

They use parts of trees to

build their homes there.
Beavers live on ponds. ∧A

beaver can use its teeth to

Then the tree falls.
gnaw on a tree.∧

Beaver Lodges
by Sean McDonald

Beavers live on ponds. They use parts of trees to build their homes there. A beaver can use its teeth to gnaw on a tree. Then the tree falls. Beavers float logs to a place to build a lodge. The beaver uses mud and grass to fill cracks. That makes the lodge warm.

Reading as a Writer

Which details did Sean add to tell more about his main idea? Where can you add details to your own paragraph?

I added more details about beavers' homes.

The Ugly Vegetables by Grace Lin

They Really Are GIANT!

☑ TARGET VOCABULARY

blooming

shovels

scent

tough

wrinkled

plain

muscles

nodded

Vocabulary Reader

The Three Sisters

Context Cards

COMMON CORE

LACC.2.L.3.6 use words and phrases acquired through conversations, reading and being read to, and responding to texts

Go Digital

Vocabulary in Context

▶ Read each **Context Card**.

▶ Make up a new sentence that uses a Vocabulary word.

1 **blooming**

Sunflowers are blooming in the field. They face the sun as their flowers grow.

2 **shovels**

These children use shovels to help plant a tree.

3 scent

Roses have a scent, or smell, that is as sweet as perfume.

4 tough

A pumpkin has a tough outer skin that is hard to break.

5 wrinkled

A raisin is a dried, wrinkled grape, but it is still sweet.

6 plain

The plant on the left is plain. The plant on the right is fancy.

7 muscles

It takes strong muscles to use a loaded wheelbarrow.

8 nodded

The girl nodded her head up and down to show that she would help in the garden.

Read and Comprehend

✅ **TARGET SKILL**

Conclusions As you read *The Ugly Vegetables,* use story clues, or text evidence, to figure out more about the events and characters. Use the clues to draw **conclusions,** or make smart guesses, about what the author does not say. You can find clues in the words and pictures. You can write the clues and a conclusion in a chart like this.

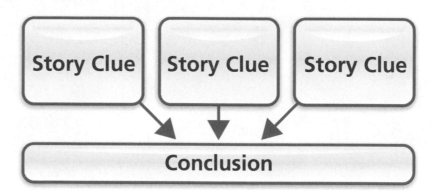

✅ **TARGET STRATEGY**

Analyze/Evaluate To **analyze** as you read, think about the author's words and story events. Then **evaluate,** or decide, how the words and events help you know what is important in the story.

COMMON CORE **LACC.2.RL.3.7** use information from illustrations and words to demonstrate understanding of characters, setting, or plot

224

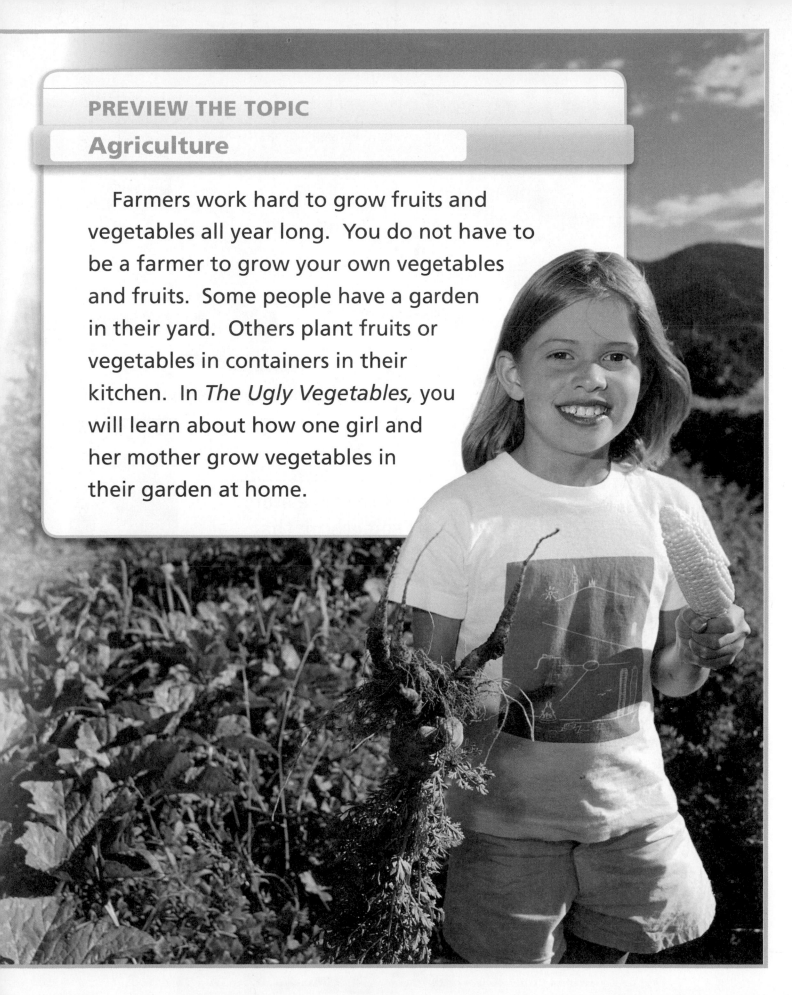

Agriculture

Farmers work hard to grow fruits and vegetables all year long. You do not have to be a farmer to grow your own vegetables and fruits. Some people have a garden in their yard. Others plant fruits or vegetables in containers in their kitchen. In *The Ugly Vegetables,* you will learn about how one girl and her mother grow vegetables in their garden at home.

The Ugly Vegetables
by Grace Lin

Conclusions Use details to figure out more about the text.

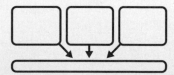

Realistic fiction is a story that could really happen. As you read, look for:

► characters who act like real people
► a problem that a real person might have

COMMON CORE   **LACC.2.RL.2.5** describe the overall structure of a story; **LACC.2.RL.3.7** use information from illustrations and words to demonstrate understanding of characters, setting, or plot; **LACC.2.RL.4.10** read and comprehend literature

 Go Digital

MEET THE AUTHOR AND ILLUSTRATOR

Grace Lin

The Ugly Vegetables tells the true story of something that happened to Grace Lin when she was little. The book caused a big problem in her family because she didn't include her two sisters in it.

They made her promise to put them in her other books, which she has done. *Dim Sum for Everyone* and *Kite Flying* are about a family with three girls, just like the Lin family.

The Ugly Vegetables

by Grace Lin

ESSENTIAL QUESTION

What can you learn from planting a garden?

In the spring I helped my mother start our garden.
We used tall shovels to turn the grass upside down, and
I saw pink worms wriggle around. It was hard work.
When we stopped to rest, we saw that the neighbors were
starting their gardens too.

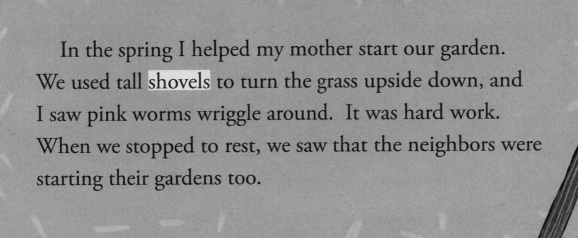

"Hello, Irma!" my mother called to Mrs. Crumerine. Mrs. Crumerine was digging too. She was using a small shovel, one that fit in her hand.

"Mommy," I asked, "why are we using such big shovels? Mrs. Crumerine has a small one."

"Because our garden needs more digging," she said.

I helped my mother plant the seeds, and we dragged the hose to the garden.

"Hi, Linda! Hi, Mickey!" I called to the Fitzgeralds. They were sprinkling water on their garden with green watering cans.

"Mommy," I asked, "why are we using a hose? Linda and Mickey use watering cans."

"Because our garden needs more water," she said.

ANALYZE THE TEXT

Conclusions What can you tell about the people in this neighborhood? Explain your answer.

Then my mother drew funny pictures on pieces of paper, and I stuck them into the garden.

"Hello, Roseanne!" my mother called across the street to Mrs. Angelhowe.

"Mommy," I asked, "why are we sticking these papers in the garden? Mrs. Angelhowe has seed packages in her garden."

"Because our garden is going to grow Chinese vegetables," she told me. "These are the names of the vegetables in Chinese, so I can tell which plants are growing where."

One day I saw our garden growing. Little green stems that looked like grass had popped out from the ground.

"Our garden's growing!" I yelled. "Our garden's growing!"

I rushed over to the neighbors' gardens to see if theirs had grown. Their plants looked like little leaves.

"Mommy," I asked, "why do our plants look like grass? The neighbors' plants look different."

"Because they are growing flowers," she said.

"Why can't we grow flowers?" I asked.

"These are better than flowers," she said.

Soon all the neighbors' gardens were blooming. Up
and down the street grew rainbows of flowers.

The wind always smelled sweet, and butterflies and
bees flew everywhere. Everyone's garden was beautiful,
except for ours.

Ours was all dark green and ugly.

"Why didn't we grow flowers?" I asked again.

"These are better than flowers," Mommy said again.

I looked, but saw only black-purple-green vines, fuzzy wrinkled leaves, prickly stems, and a few little yellow flowers.

"I don't think so," I said.

"You wait and see," Mommy said.

Before long, our vegetables grew. Some were big
and lumpy. Some were thin and green and covered with
bumps. Some were just plain icky yellow. They were
ugly vegetables.

Sometimes I would go over to the neighbors' and
look at their pretty gardens. They would show the
poppies and peonies and petunias to me, and I would feel
sad that our garden wasn't as nice.

One day my mother and I picked the vegetables from the garden. We filled a whole wheelbarrow full of them. We wheeled them to the kitchen. My mother washed them and took a big knife and started to chop them.

"Aie-yow!" she said when she cut them. She had to use all her muscles. The vegetables were hard and tough.

"This is sheau hwang gua (show hwang gwa)," Mommy said, handing me a bumpy, curled vegetable. She pointed at the other vegetables. "This is shiann tsay (shen zai). That's a torng hau (tung how)."

I went outside to play. While I was playing catch
with Mickey, a magical aroma filled the air. I saw the
neighbors standing on their porches with their eyes closed,
smelling the sky. They took deep breaths of air, like they
were trying to eat the smell.

The wind carried it up and down the street. Even
the bees and the butterflies seemed to smell the scent
in the breeze.

I smelled it too. It made me hungry, and it was coming from my house!

When I followed it to my house, my mother was putting a big bowl of soup on the table. The soup was yellow and red and green and pink.

"This is a special soup," Mommy said, and she smiled.

She gave me a small bowl full of it and I tasted it. It was so good! The flavors of the soup seemed to dance in my mouth and laugh all the way down to my stomach. I smiled.

"Do you like it?" Mommy asked me.

I nodded and held out my bowl for some more.

"It's made from our vegetables," she told me.

Then the doorbell rang, and we ran to open the door.

All our neighbors were standing at the door holding flowers.

"We noticed you were cooking." Mr. Fitzgerald laughed as he held out his flowers. "And we thought maybe you might be interested in a trade!"

We laughed too, and my mother gave them each their
own bowl of her special soup.

My mother told them what each vegetable was and
how she grew it. She gave them the soup recipe and put
some soup into jars for them to take home. I ate five
bowls of soup.

It was the best dinner ever.

The next spring, when my mother was starting her garden, we planted some flowers next to the Chinese vegetables. Mrs. Crumerine, the Fitzgeralds, and the Angelhowes planted some Chinese vegetables next to their flowers.

Soon the whole neighborhood was growing Chinese vegetables in their gardens. Up and down the street, little green plants poked out of the ground. Some looked like leaves and some looked like grass, and when the flowers started blooming, you could smell soup in the air.

ANALYZE THE TEXT

Story Structure How is the neighborhood different at the end of the story than at the beginning of the story?

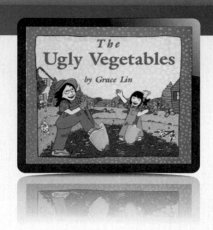

Dig Deeper

How to Analyze the Text

Use these pages to learn about Conclusions and Story Structure. Then read *The Ugly Vegetables* again. Use what you learn to understand it better.

Conclusions

The Ugly Vegetables is a story about a girl and her garden. The author does not tell when and where the story takes place. You must find clues in the story and pictures to draw **conclusions** about the setting. When you draw conclusions, you make smart guesses about what the author does not say.

The words and pictures in a story are text evidence that can help you draw conclusions. Use a chart like this.

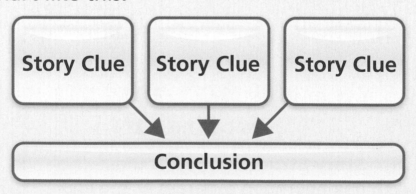

LACC.2.RL.2.5 describe the overall structure of a story; **LACC.2.RL.3.7** use information from illustrations and words to demonstrate understanding of characters, setting, or plot

250

Story Structure

Characters are the people in a story. The **setting** is where and when the story takes place. The **plot** is what happens in the story. The beginning explains who the characters are, when and where the story takes place, and what the main problem is. The ending tells how the problem is solved. All of the story parts make up the **story structure**.

Your Turn

What can you learn from planting a garden? Use evidence from the story to help you talk about your ideas with a partner. Take turns speaking and listening. Remember to speak in complete sentences.

Classroom Conversation

Now talk about these questions with the class.

1 What text evidence does the author give to help you figure out the setting?

2 How do you think Mommy learned to make the soup?

3 Why did the author write this story? Use text evidence from the story to explain.

WRITE ABOUT READING

Response Write sentences to tell how the girl's garden is different from the neighbors' gardens. Then draw a picture of each garden. Use the words and pictures from the story to help you.

Writing Tip

Use describing words to help show what each garden is like.

COMMON CORE **LACC.2.RL.3.7** use information from illustrations and words to demonstrate understanding of characters, setting, or plot; **LACC.2.W.1.2** write informative/explanatory texts; **LACC.2.SL.1.1.a** follow rules for discussions; **LACC.2.SL.2.6** produce complete sentences to provide detail or clarification

INFORMATIONAL TEXT

☑ GENRE

Informational text gives facts about a topic. This is a magazine article.

☑ TEXT FOCUS

A **bar graph** is a drawing that uses bars to compare numbers.

They Really Are GIANT!

by Judy Williams

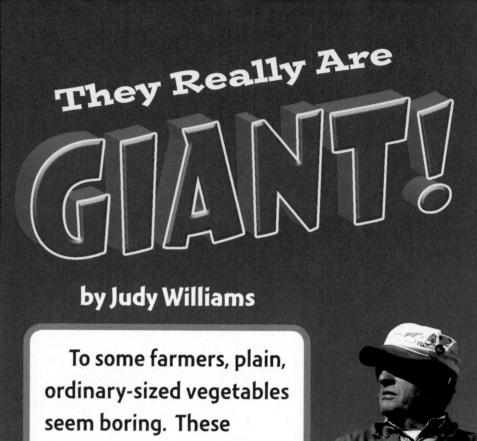

To some farmers, plain, ordinary-sized vegetables seem boring. These farmers think big. They like to grow the biggest vegetables ever.

COMMON CORE LACC.2.RI.3.7 explain how images contribute to and clarify text; LACC.2.RI.4.10 read and comprehend informational texts

Go Digital

World Record Breakers

Plants are always blooming in California. The scent of rich soil fills the air. Every year in Half Moon Bay, the town holds the World Championship Pumpkin Weigh-Off. The judges all nodded yes when they saw the 2007 winner. It weighed 1,524 pounds, more than a big horse!

Pumpkins aren't the only giant veggies though. Some farmers use their muscles and heavy shovels to dig up 30-pound beets and turnips. Although these giants look tough, they are tender and delicious to eat.

Thadd Starr won first prize at the Half Moon Bay contest for his super-sized pumpkin.

Home of the Giants

Alaska might be the home of giant veggies. More giant vegetables seem to grow there than any other place in the world. Long summer days and good soil make veggies grow and grow. You can see 98-pound cabbages at the Alaska State Fair in Palmer.

Seven-year-old Brenna Dinkel from Wasilla, Alaska, looks small next to this giant wrinkled leaf cabbage!

How Big Are They?

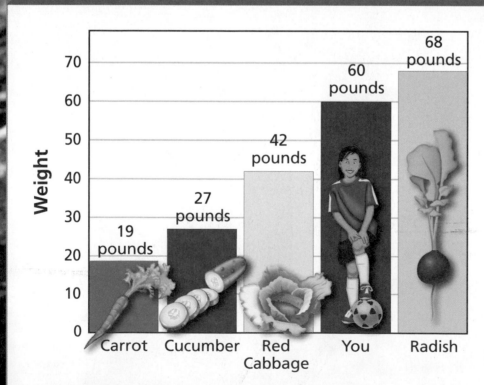

Weight

Carrot	Cucumber	Red Cabbage	You	Radish
19 pounds	27 pounds	42 pounds	60 pounds	68 pounds

Compare Texts

Compare and Contrast Compare what you learned about the different types of plants in the two selections. Discuss your ideas with a partner. Be sure to speak in complete sentences.

Share Experiences List the steps that the characters take to plant and care for their vegetables in *The Ugly Vegetables*. Which step do you think is the most important? Why?

Connect to Social Studies In *The Ugly Vegetables*, Mommy says she is growing Chinese vegetables. Find China on a map or globe. Talk with a partner about what you found.

COMMON CORE **LACC.2.RI.3.9** compare and contrast points presented by two texts on same topic; **LACC.2.SL.2.6** produce complete sentences to provide detail or clarification

Grammar

Proper Nouns **Proper nouns** are the special names of people, animals, places, or things. Proper nouns begin with **capital letters**.

Nouns	Proper Nouns
neighbor	Carissa Smith
pet	Fluffy
road	Main Street
drink	So Fruity Punch
state	Florida
country	China

Try This! **Write each sentence correctly. Remember to begin each proper noun with a capital letter.**

❶ There are many gardens in centerville.

❷ My friend molly bowen picked apples.

❸ mei's favorite toy is called action king.

A proper noun names a special person, animal, place, or thing. A proper noun is one kind of exact noun. Use exact nouns in your writing to paint a picture in your reader's mind.

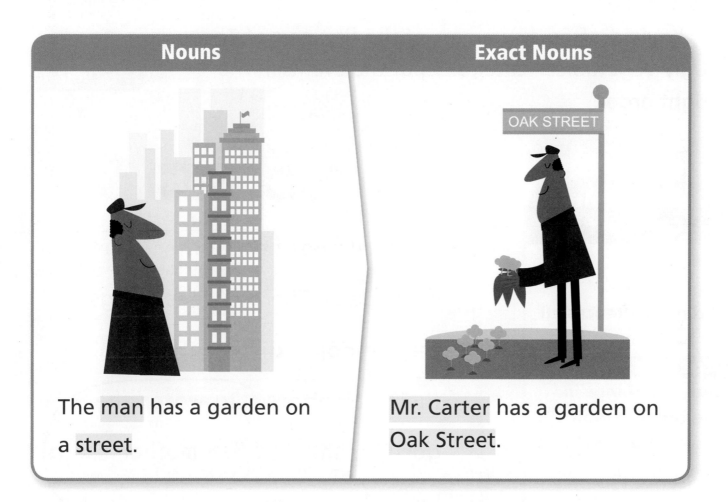

Nouns	Exact Nouns
The man has a garden on a street.	Mr. Carter has a garden on Oak Street.

 ## Connect Grammar to Writing

When you revise your summary paragraph, look for nouns you can change to exact nouns. Be sure to begin each proper noun with a capital letter.

Informative Writing

☑ **Organization** A **summary** tells what happens in a story by putting the events in the same order as they happened.

Kayla drafted a summary of the first part of *The Ugly Vegetables*. Later, she put the events in the right order.

Writing Traits Checklist

☑ **Idea**
Did my sentences all tie to the main idea?

☑ **Organization**
Did I tell things in the order in which they happened?

☑ **Sentence Fluency**
Are the words in my sentences in an order that makes sense?

☑ **Conventions**
Did I capitalize and punctuate my sentences correctly?

Revised Draft

A girl helps her mother start a garden. The girl sees things they're doing differently from their neighbors. To water the garden, she and her mother use a hose. The neighbors use watering cans. The neighbors use smaller shovels.

260

My Summary
by Kayla Higgs

A girl helps her mother start a garden. The girl sees things they're doing differently from their neighbors. The neighbors use smaller shovels. To water the garden, she and her mother use a hose. The neighbors use watering cans.

The girl asks why their garden is different from the neighbors' gardens. Her mother says the vegetables they are growing are better than flowers. The girl doesn't believe her until the end of the story!

Reading as a Writer

Why did Kayla move sentences? What can you move in your writing to put events in the right order?

I moved sentences around to tell things in the order in which they happened.

Lesson

8

✓ **TARGET VOCABULARY**

beware

damage

bend

flash

pounding

prevent

reach

equal

Vocabulary Reader

Context Cards

COMMON CORE **LACC.2.L.3.6** use words and phrases acquired through conversations, reading and being read to, and responding to texts

Vocabulary in Context

▶ Read each **Context Card**.

▶ Talk about a picture. Use a different Vocabulary word from the one on the card.

---

1 **beware**

Beware of dangerous weather when a storm siren sounds its warning.

---

2 **damage**

Hail and strong winds can do a lot of harm. They can damage crops.

3 bend

High winds have caused the trunks of these trees to bend, or curve.

4 flash

The flash of lightning bolts lit up the dark night sky.

5 pounding

Pounding waves hit the beach hard in a storm.

6 prevent

Heavy snow may prevent, or stop, cars and trucks from traveling.

7 reach

In a flood, water can reach, or go as high as, rooftops.

8 equal

The height of the snow is equal to three feet.

Read and Comprehend

 Go Digital

☑ **TARGET SKILL**

Main Idea and Details The **topic** of an informational text is what the text is about. **Main ideas** are the most important ideas about the topic. **Details** tell more about each main idea. Use a chart like this to list main ideas and details.

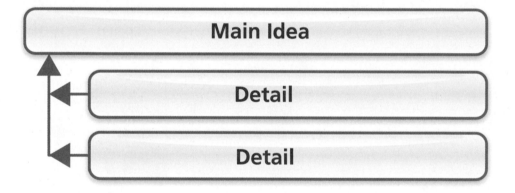

| Main Idea |
| Detail |
| Detail |

☑ **TARGET STRATEGY**

Visualize As you read, picture what is happening to help you understand and remember important ideas and details.

Do you ever wonder about the weather? Most people like when the weather is sunny. Sometimes, though, the weather can cause problems. When it rains or snows, you may have to stay inside. Some weather can even be dangerous. Tornadoes and hurricanes are two kinds of dangerous storms.

You will read about some types of dangerous weather in *Super Storms*.

ANCHOR TEXT

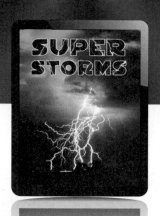

SUPER STORMS

SEYMOUR SIMON

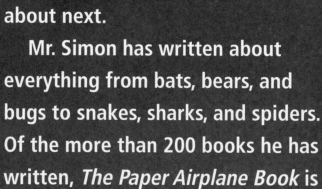

As a former science teacher, Seymour Simon loves to visit classrooms and talk with students. Those visits sometimes help him decide what to write about next.

Mr. Simon has written about everything from bats, bears, and bugs to snakes, sharks, and spiders. Of the more than 200 books he has written, *The Paper Airplane Book* is one of his favorites.

 TARGET SKILL

Main Idea and Details Tell important ideas and details about a topic.

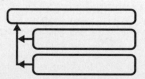

 GENRE

Informational text gives facts about a topic. As you read, look for:

▸ photos
▸ facts and details about a topic
▸ maps or charts that help explain the topic

LACC.2.RI.1.2 identify the main topic of a multiparagraph text and the focus of specific paragraphs; **LACC.2.RI.1.3** describe the connection between a series of historical events/scientific ideas/ steps in technical procedures

COMMON CORE

 Go Digital

SUPER STORMS

by Seymour Simon

ESSENTIAL QUESTION

How can some storms
be dangerous?

The air around us is always moving and changing. We call these changes weather. Storms are sudden, violent changes in weather.

Every second, hundreds of thunderstorms
are born around the world. Thunderstorms are
heavy rain showers. They can drop millions of
gallons of water in just one minute.

During a thunderstorm, lightning bolts can shoot between clouds and the ground. Lightning can destroy a tree or a small house. It can also start fires in forests and grasslands.

Thunder is the sound lightning makes as it suddenly heats the air. You can tell how far away lightning is. Count the seconds between the flash of light and the sound of thunder. Five seconds equal one mile.

Hailstones are chunks of ice that are tossed up and down by the winds of some thunderstorms. Hail can be the size of a marble or larger than a baseball. Nearly 5,000 hailstorms strike the United States every year. They can destroy crops and damage buildings and cars.

Thunderstorms sometimes give birth to tornadoes. Inside a storm, a funnel-shaped cloud reaches downward. Winds inside a tornado can spin faster than 300 miles per hour. These winds can lift cars off the ground and rip houses apart.

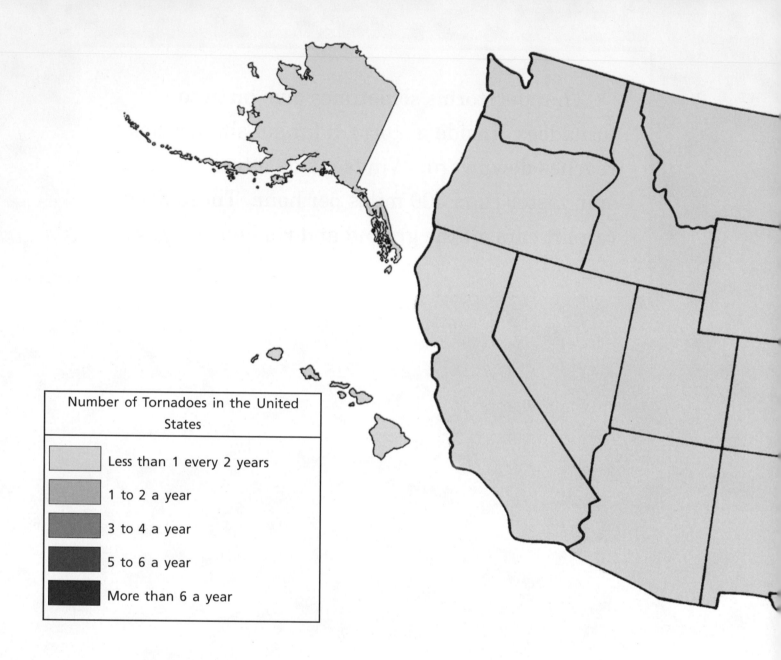

Number of Tornadoes in the United States

	Less than 1 every 2 years
	1 to 2 a year
	3 to 4 a year
	5 to 6 a year
	More than 6 a year

More than 1,000 tornadoes strike the United States each year. Most of them form during spring and summer.

Television and radio stations often give early alerts. A tornado watch means that one may strike during the next few hours. A warning means a tornado has been seen by people or on radar. During a tornado warning you should find shelter in a basement or closet.

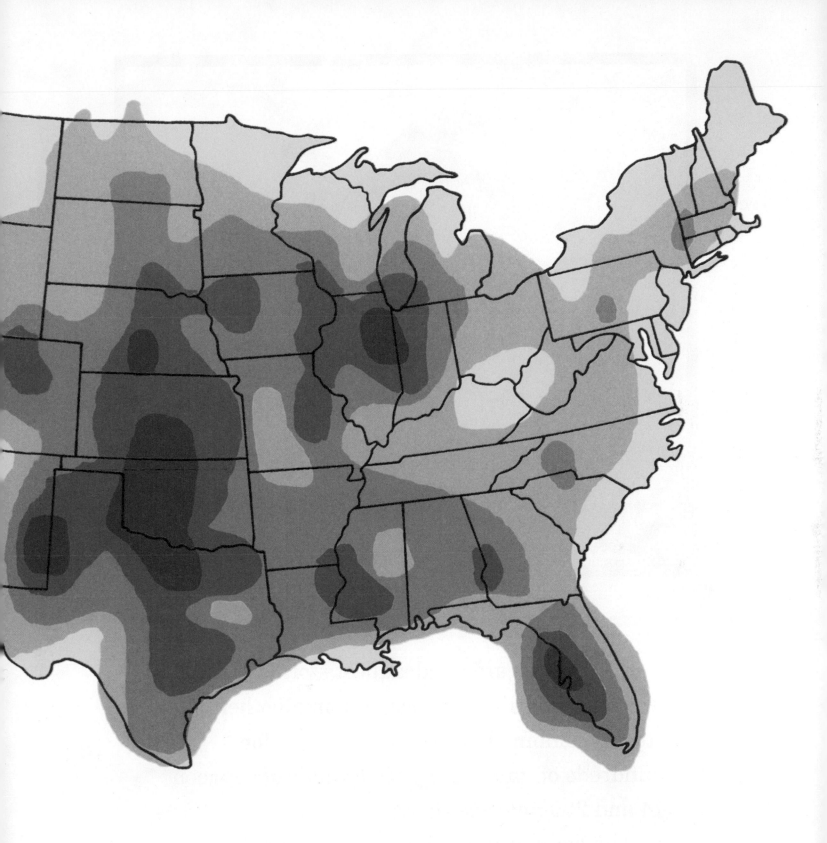

Hurricanes are the deadliest storms in the world. They kill more people than all other storms combined. Hurricanes stretch for hundreds of miles. They have winds of between 74 and 200 miles per hour.

The eye of a hurricane is the quiet center of the storm. Inside the eye, the wind stops blowing, the sun shines, and the sky is blue. But beware, the storm is not over yet.

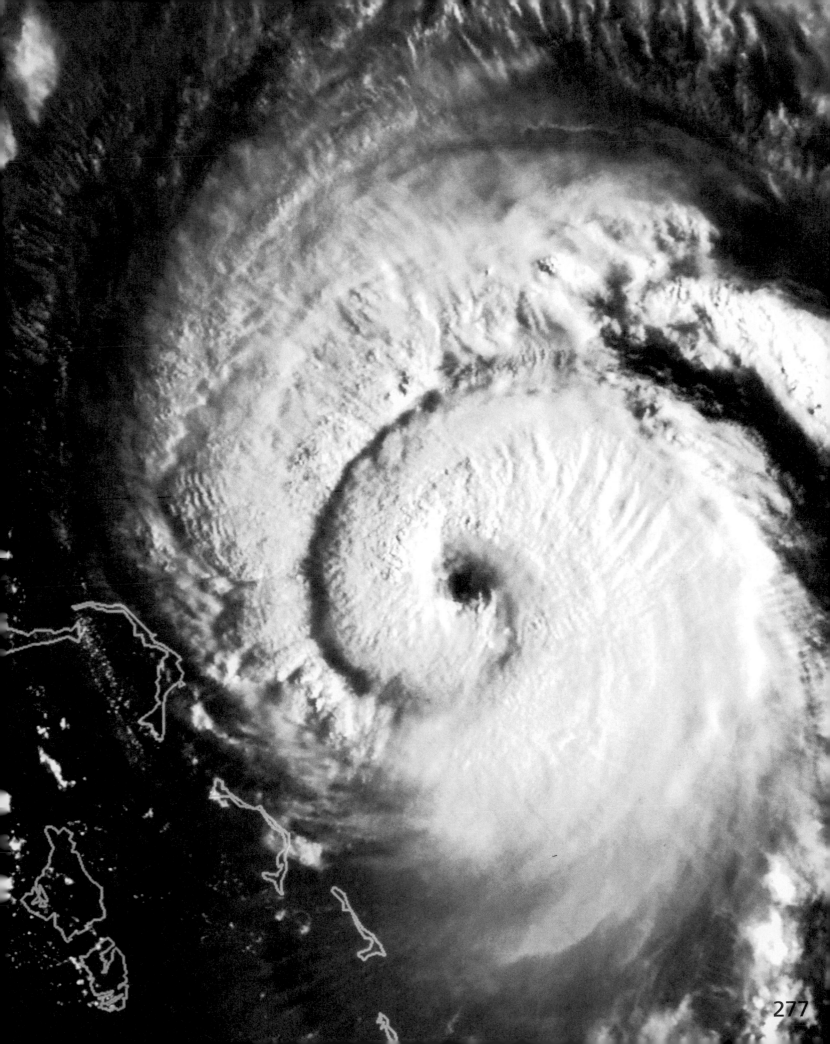

Hurricanes are born over warm ocean waters from early summer to mid-fall. When they finally reach land, their pounding waves wash away beaches, boats, and houses. Their howling winds bend and uproot trees and telephone poles. Their heavy rains cause floods.

Blizzards are huge snowstorms. They have winds of at least 35 miles per hour. Usually at least two inches of snow falls per hour. Temperatures are at 20 degrees or lower. Falling and blowing snow make it hard to see in a blizzard.

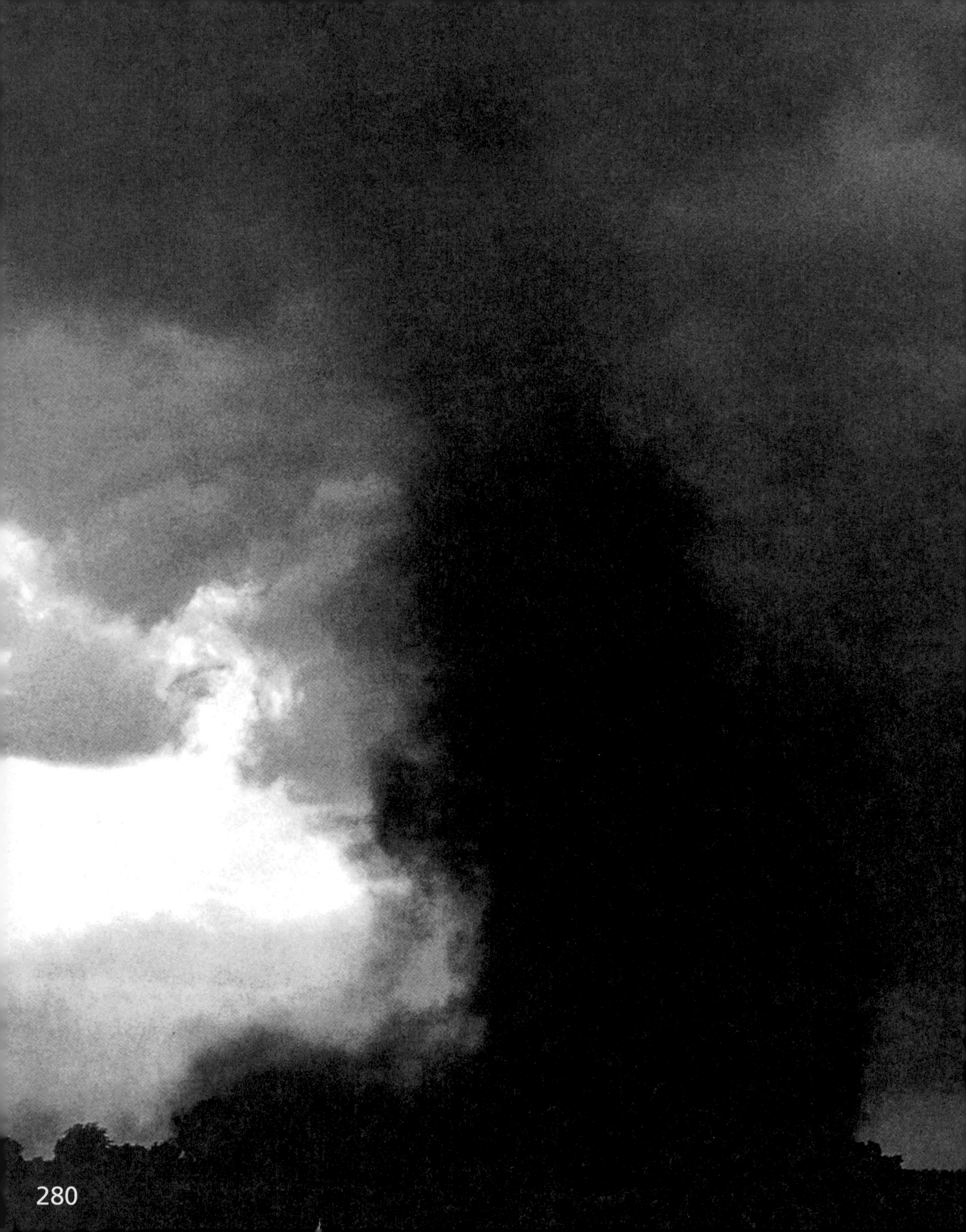

No one can prevent storms. But weather reports can predict and warn us when a storm may hit. The more prepared we are, the safer we will be when the next one strikes.

ANALYZE THE TEXT

Main Idea and Details What is the topic of *Super Storms*? What is the main idea?

Dig Deeper

How to Analyze the Text

Use these pages to learn about Main Idea and Details and Cause and Effect. Then read *Super Storms* again. Use what you learn to understand it better.

Main Idea and Details

The author of *Super Storms* wrote about one main topic. He included a main idea and details in each section that explain the topic. The **main idea** is the most important idea in each section. **Details** tell you more information about the main idea. As you reread, use a chart like the one below. Record each main idea and the details that tell more about it.

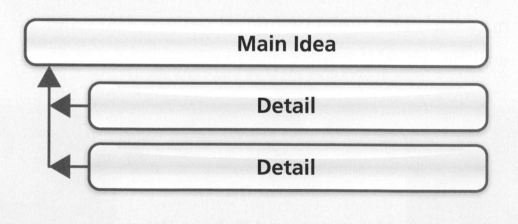

LACC.2.RI.1.2 identify the main topic of a multiparagraph text and the focus of specific paragraphs; **LACC.2.RI.1.3** describe the connection between a series of historical events/scientific ideas/steps in technical procedures

Cause and Effect

When one thing makes another happen, it is called cause and effect. For example, the wind of a tornado can make trees fall over. The tornado is the **cause**. Trees falling over is the **effect**. When you read, ask yourself what happens and why. This can help you understand how ideas are connected.

Your Turn

RETURN TO THE ESSENTIAL QUESTION

Turn and Talk

How can some storms be dangerous?
Use text evidence from *Super Storms* in your answer. Share your ideas with a partner. Remember to use respectful ways to take your turn speaking.

Classroom Conversation

Now talk about these questions with the class.

1. Which details in the selection help you figure out the topic and main idea?

2. How do the photos help you understand more about each storm?

3. Look back at page 279. What is the main idea of this section? What details tell more about it?

Response Which type of weather do you think is the scariest? Write a few sentences to tell why. Use text evidence to help explain your opinion.

Writing Tip

Join two sentences that have the same predicate. Remember to use *and* between the two subjects.

LACC.2.RI.1.2 identify the main topic of a multiparagraph text and the focus of specific paragraphs; **LACC.2.W.1.1** write opinion pieces; **LACC.2.SL.1.1.a** follow rules for discussions; **LACC.2.L.1.1.f** produce, expand, and rearrange complete simple and compound sentences

POETRY

Weather Poems

✓ GENRE

Poetry uses the sound of words to show pictures and feelings.

✓ TEXT FOCUS

Repetition is when the same words are used more than once.

Weather Poems

Many poets write poems about the weather. They might write about a flash of lightning or the way wind bends flowers.

The three poems you will read next are about the weather. Listen to the words that repeat in the poem "Night Drumming for Rain." Does it remind you of pounding raindrops?

LACC.2.RL.2.4 describe how words and phrases supply rhythm and meaning; **LACC.2.RL.4.10** read and comprehend literature

Night Drumming for Rain

hi-iya nai-ho-o

earth rumbling

earth rumbling

our basket drum sounding

earth rumbling

everywhere humming

everywhere raining

Pima

Who Has Seen the Wind?

Who has seen the wind?

   Neither I nor you.

But when the leaves hang trembling,

   The wind is passing through.

Who has seen the wind?

   Neither you nor I.

But when the trees bow down their heads,

   The wind is passing by.

by Christina G. Rossetti

287

Weather

Dot a dot dot   dot a dot dot
Spotting the windowpane.
Spack a spack speck   flick a flack fleck
Freckling the windowpane.

A spatter a scatter   a wet cat a clatter
A splatter a rumble outside.
Umbrella umbrella umbrella umbrella
Bumbershoot barrel of rain.

Slosh a galosh   slosh a galosh
Slither and slather and glide
A puddle a jump a puddle a jump
A puddle a jump puddle splosh
A juddle a pump aluddle a dump a
Puddmuddle jump in and slide!

by Eve Merriam

Write a Weather Poem

Write your own weather poem. Include words that repeat more than once. You might describe a hot summer day. You might write about how you feel when it rains. You might even write a funny poem about getting caught in a storm!

Compare Texts

TEXT TO TEXT

Understand Poems Read the poems in *Weather Poems* again with a partner. Which poems use repeated words to help the reader understand what the author wants to say? Which ones use rhythm? Do any of them rhyme? Take turns speaking and listening.

TEXT TO SELF

Make a Plan Choose one type of storm from *Super Storms*. With the class, talk about what you would do to stay safe during that kind of weather. Speak only when it is your turn.

TEXT TO WORLD

Observe Local Weather What types of weather from *Super Storms* or *Weather Poems* do you get where you live? List each type. Compare your list with a partner's.

COMMON CORE **LACC.2.RL.2.4** describe how words and phrases supply rhythm and meaning; **LACC.2.SL.1.1.a** follow rules for discussions

Grammar

What Is a Verb? A **verb** names an action that someone or something does or did. A verb is found in the action part, or **predicate,** of a sentence.

Verbs in Sentences

Rain falls.

Strong winds blow.

The storm destroyed homes.

The tornado bent many trees.

 **Work with a partner. Read the sentences aloud. Name the verb in each sentence.**

1. I learned about storms.

2. We stay indoors.

3. Tornadoes form in summer.

4. The thunder scared my cat.

When you write, use exact verbs. They make your sentences come alive and tell your reader exactly what is happening.

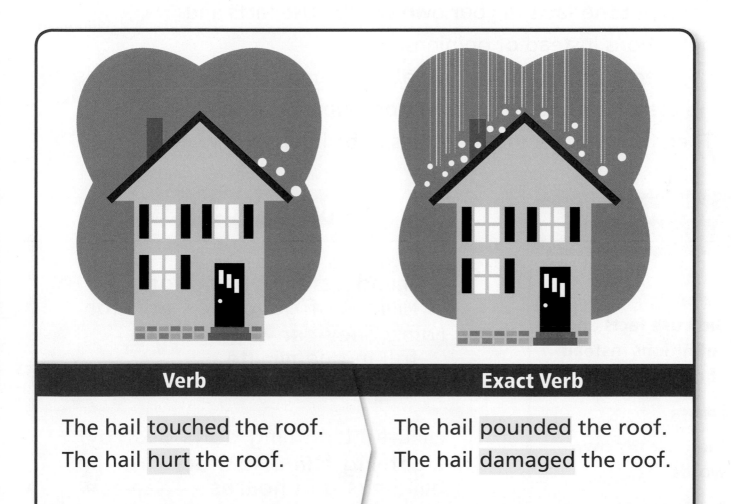

Verb	Exact Verb
The hail touched the roof.	The hail pounded the roof.
The hail hurt the roof.	The hail damaged the roof.

 ## Connect Grammar to Writing

When you revise your writing, look for verbs that you can change to more exact verbs.

Informative Writing

☑ **Voice** When you write an **informational paragraph,** think about the facts you want to include. Then put the facts in your own words. Use facts and definitions instead of opinions.

Greg drafted a paragraph about thunderstorms. He used facts and definitions from *Super Storms.* Then he revised some sentences to be in his own words.

Writing Traits Checklist

☑ **Ideas**
Did I use facts and definitions instead of opinions?

☑ **Voice**
Did I use my own words?

☑ **Sentence Fluency**
Did I get rid of short, choppy sentences?

☑ **Conventions**
Did I write neatly and leave margins?

Revised Draft

Thunderstorms bring lots of
Millions of gallons of rain can
rain. ∧ ~~They can drop millions~~
fall in one minute.
~~of gallons of water in just one~~

~~minute.~~ Lightning bolts destroy
Lightning can also start fires in
buildings and houses. ∧ ~~They can~~
trees or grass!
~~also start fires in forests and~~
Thunder is the sound made when
~~grasslands. Thunder is the sound~~
lightning he∧ats the air quickly.
~~lightning makes as it suddenly~~

~~heats the air.~~

292

Thunderstorms
by Greg Popov

Thunderstorms bring lots of rain. Millions of gallons of rain can fall in one minute. Lightning bolts destroy buildings and houses. Lightning can also start fires in trees or grass! Thunder is the sound made when lightning heats the air quickly. People can tell how close lightning is by counting the seconds between lightning and the sound of thunder. For every five seconds you count, the lightning is one mile away. Try this the next time you see lightning!

Reading as a Writer

How did Greg tell facts in his own words? Where did he use definitions? Where can you use definitions in your writing?

I made sure I used my own words to tell facts.

How Chipmunk Got His Stripes

Joseph Bruchac & James Bruchac
Pictures by Jose Aruego
& Ariane Dewey

Why Rabbits Have Short Tails

☑ **TARGET VOCABULARY**

tunnel

curled

height

direction

toward

healed

brag

tease

**Vocabulary
Reader**

Native American
Folktales

**Context
Cards**

tunnel

A chipmunk knows how to dig a tunnel, which is a passage underground.

COMMON
CORE

LACC.2.L.3.6 use words and phrases acquired through conversations, reading and being read to, and responding to texts

Go
Digital

Vocabulary in Context

► Read each **Context Card**.

► Ask a question that uses one of the Vocabulary words.

1

tunnel

A chipmunk knows how to dig a tunnel, which is a passage underground.

2

curled

This fox is curled up around its warm, bushy tail.

3 height

An eagle builds its nest at an amazing height. It is at the top of a tall tree.

4 direction

An owl can turn its head in any direction. It can look all around.

5 toward

These bear cubs run toward their mother so she can protect them.

6 healed

This pangolin will go back to the forest when it is well, or healed.

7 brag

These antlers are something to brag about! They are huge.

8 tease

Never tease, or bother, wild animals. Always respect them.

Read and Comprehend

✓ **TARGET SKILL**

Understanding Characters In *How Chipmunk Got His Stripes,* the characters Bear and Brown Squirrel speak and act like people. Think about what they say, think, and do when something happens to them in the story. Paying attention to this text evidence can help you understand what each character is like.

Use a chart to list the characters and your ideas.

Character	Event	Words, Thoughts, Actions

✓ **TARGET STRATEGY**

Summarize Stop to tell important events as you read.

 COMMON CORE **LACC.2.RL.1.2** recount stories and determine their message, lesson, or moral; **LACC.2.RL.1.3** describe how characters respond to events and challenges

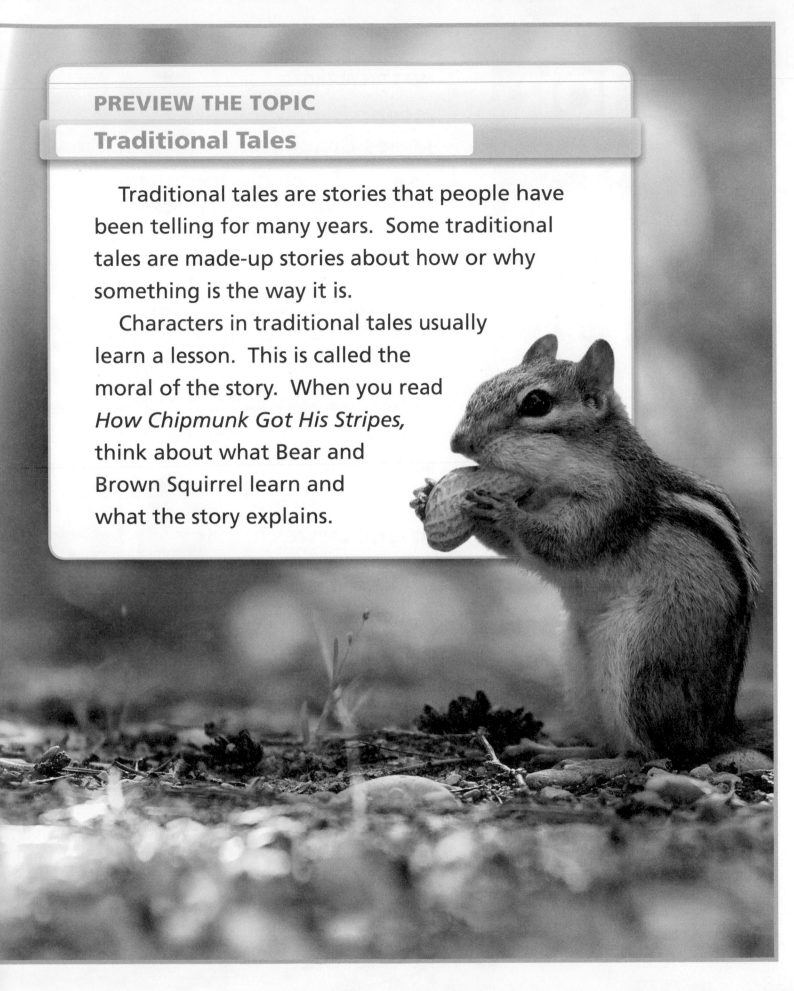

Traditional Tales

Traditional tales are stories that people have been telling for many years. Some traditional tales are made-up stories about how or why something is the way it is.

Characters in traditional tales usually learn a lesson. This is called the moral of the story. When you read *How Chipmunk Got His Stripes,* think about what Bear and Brown Squirrel learn and what the story explains.

ANCHOR TEXT

How Chipmunk Got His Stripes
Joseph Bruchac & James Bruchac
Pictures by Jose Aruego
& Ariane Dewey

✓ TARGET SKILL

Understanding Characters Tell more about characters.

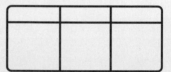

✓ GENRE

A **folktale** is a kind of traditional tale. As you read, look for:

▶ a simple plot that teaches a lesson

▶ animal characters who talk and act like people

COMMON CORE

LACC.2.RL.1.3 describe how characters respond to events and challenges; **LACC.2.RL.2.4** describe how words and phrases supply rhythm and meaning; **LACC.2.RL.4.10** read and comprehend literature

 Go Digital

MEET THE AUTHORS

Joseph Bruchac and James Bruchac

As a boy, Joseph Bruchac listened to his grandfather tell stories of their Native American heritage. Joseph passed these stories down to his son, James. Now this father-and-son team writes books together, such as *Raccoon's Last Race*.

MEET THE ILLUSTRATORS

Jose Aruego and Ariane Dewey

These two artists make a great team. When they are working on a book, Jose Aruego first draws the lines for the characters, using pen and ink. Then Ariane Dewey paints the colors. In this way, they have illustrated more than 60 books.

How Chipmunk Got His Stripes

by Joseph Bruchac and James Bruchac

pictures by Jose Aruego and Ariane Dewey

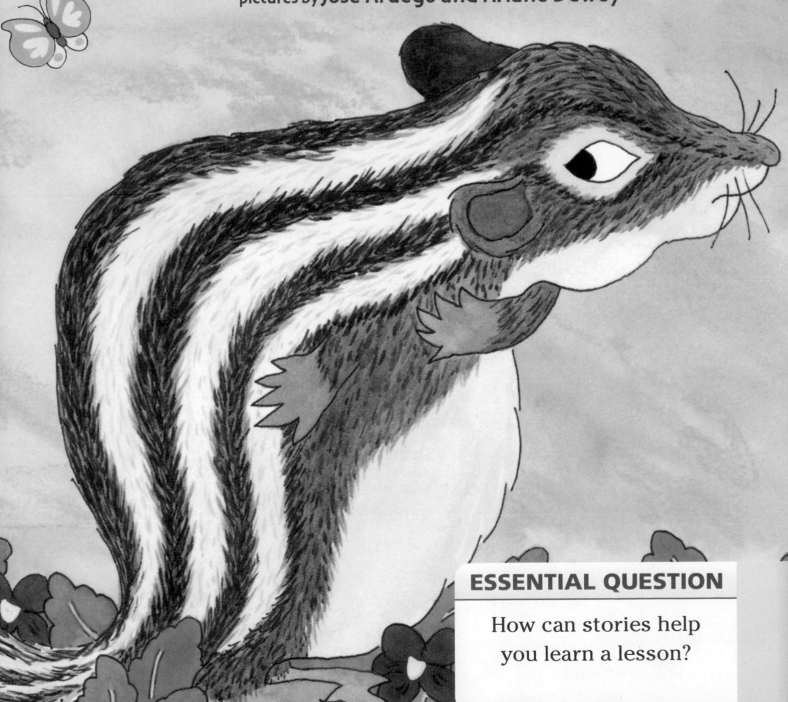

ESSENTIAL QUESTION

How can stories help you learn a lesson?

One autumn day long ago, Bear was out walking.
As he walked, he began to brag:

"I am Bear. I am the biggest
of all the animals. Yes, I am!
I am Bear. I am the strongest
of all the animals. Yes, I am!
I am Bear. I am the loudest
of all the animals. Yes, I am!
I am Bear, I am Bear.
I can do anything. Yes, I can!"

As soon as Bear said those words, a little voice spoke up from the ground.

"Can you really do anything?"

Bear looked down. He saw a little brown squirrel, standing on his hind legs.

"Can you really do anything?" Brown Squirrel asked again.

Bear stood up very tall. "I am Bear. I can do anything. Yes, I can!"

"Can you tell the sun not to rise tomorrow morning?" Brown Squirrel asked.

"I have never tried that before. But I am Bear. I can do that. Yes, I can!"

ANALYZE THE TEXT

Understanding Characters What does Bear say and do? What does this tell you about him?

Bear turned west to face the sun. It was the time
when the sun always goes down. Bear stood up to his
full height and spoke in a loud voice.

"SUN, DO NOT COME UP TOMORROW."

At his words, the sun began to disappear behind
the hills.

"You see?" Bear said. "Sun is afraid of me.
He is running away."

"But will the sun come up tomorrow?"
Brown Squirrel asked.

"No," Bear answered. "The sun will not come up!"

Then Bear turned to face east, the direction where the sun always used to come up. He sat down. Little Brown Squirrel sat down beside him. All that night, they did not sleep. All that night, Bear kept saying these words:

"The sun will not come up, hummph!
The sun will not come up, hummph!"

But as the night went on, little Brown Squirrel began to say something, too. He said these words:
"The sun is going to rise, oooh!
The sun is going to rise, oooh!"

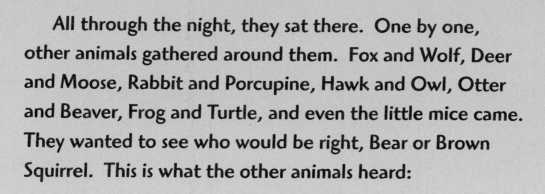

All through the night, they sat there. One by one, other animals gathered around them. Fox and Wolf, Deer and Moose, Rabbit and Porcupine, Hawk and Owl, Otter and Beaver, Frog and Turtle, and even the little mice came. They wanted to see who would be right, Bear or Brown Squirrel. This is what the other animals heard:

"The sun will not come up, hummph!"
"The sun is going to rise, oooh!"
"The sun will not come up, hummph!"
"The sun is going to rise, oooh!"

ANALYZE THE TEXT

Author's Word Choice Why does the author keep repeating Bear's sentence and little Brown Squirrel's sentence?

Finally, it was just before dawn, the time when the sun always used to come up.

"Look," said Turtle, "a little bit of red is starting to show."

"Yes," said Owl. "I believe the sun will rise today."

Bear only chanted louder:

"The sun will not come up, hummph!"

But right next to him, little Brown Squirrel piped up:

"The sun is going to rise, oooh!"

And the sun came up. The birds sang their welcoming songs. The bright light of the new day spread over the land. Everyone was happy except for one animal. That animal was Bear. He sat there with his head down and a grumpy look on his face.

The happiest animal of all was little Brown Squirrel. "The sun came up," he chirped. "The sun came up, the sun came up, the sun came up."

Brown Squirrel was so happy, he forgot what his wise old grandmother had told him when he was very young.

"Brown Squirrel," his grandmother had said, "it is good to be right about something. But when someone else is wrong, it is not a good idea to tease him."

Now little Brown Squirrel began to tease Bear.

"Bear is foolish, the sun came up.
Bear is silly, the sun came up.
Bear is stupid, the sun—"

WHOMP!

Bear's big paw came down on little Brown Squirrel, pinning him to the ground. Bear leaned over and opened his huge mouth.

"Yes," Bear growled. "The sun did come up. Yes, I do look foolish. But you will not live to see another sunrise. You will not ever tease anyone else again, because I, Bear, am going to eat you."

Brown Squirrel thought fast. "You are right to eat me," he said. "I was wrong to tease you. I would like to say I am sorry before you eat me. But you are pressing down on me so hard that I cannot say anything. I cannot say anything at all. I cannot even breathe. If you would lift up your paw just a little bit, then I could take a deep breath and apologize before you eat me."

"That is a good idea," Bear said. "I would like to hear you apologize before I eat you."

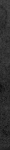

So Bear lifted up his paw. But instead of apologizing, Brown Squirrel ran. He ran as fast as he could toward the pile of stones where he had his home. He had a tunnel under those stones and a nice warm burrow underground. Little Brown Squirrel's grandmother stood there in the door waiting for him.

"Hurry, Brown Squirrel," she called. "Hurry, hurry!"

Little Brown Squirrel dove for the door to his home. But Bear was faster than he looked. He grabbed for little Brown Squirrel with his big paw. Bear's long, sharp claws scratched Brown Squirrel's back from the top of his head to the tip of his tail.

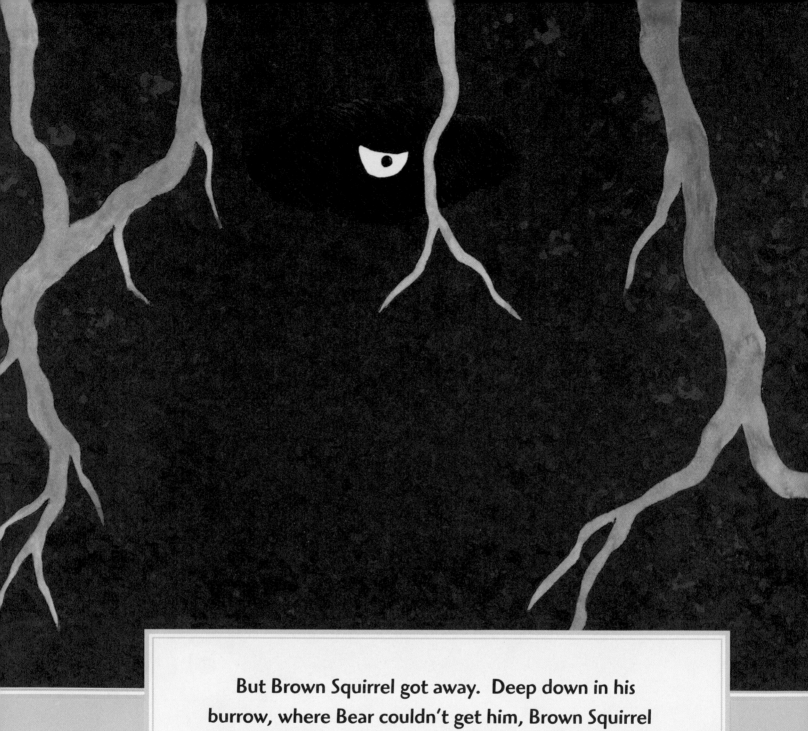

But Brown Squirrel got away. Deep down in his burrow, where Bear couldn't get him, Brown Squirrel curled up next to his grandmother and slept all winter while those scratches on his back healed.

When spring came again, little Brown Squirrel came
out of his hole and looked at himself. There were long
pale stripes all the way down his back where Bear had
scratched him. He was Brown Squirrel no longer. He was
now Chipmunk, the striped one.

That is how Chipmunk got his stripes. Ever since then, Chipmunk has been the first animal to get up every morning. As the sun rises, he scoots to the top of the tallest tree to sing his song:

"The sun came up,
the sun came up,
the sun came up,
the sun came up!"

And ever since then, Bear has been the last animal to get up. He doesn't like to hear Chipmunk's song. It reminds him—as it reminds us all—that no one, not even Bear, can do everything.

Dig Deeper

How to Analyze the Text

Use these pages to learn about Understanding Characters and Author's Word Choice. Then read *How Chipmunk Got His Stripes* again. Use what you learn to understand it better.

Understanding Characters

How Chipmunk Got His Stripes tells why chipmunks look the way they do. In this story, the characters deal with some problems. For example, Brown Squirrel tells Bear that he can't keep the sun from coming up.

Think about what the characters do and say when they have a problem. List text evidence in a chart like the one below.

Character	Event	Words, Thoughts, Actions

COMMON CORE LACC.2.RL.1.3 describe how characters respond to events and challenges; LACC.2.RL.2.4 describe how words and phrases supply rhythm and meaning

Author's Word Choice

Authors sometimes repeat words or phrases. This is called **repetition**. Repetition sometimes makes the words you read have a rhythm, or beat. Repetition also helps you understand important parts of the story. On page 300, Bear repeats, "Yes, I am!" This helps you understand that Bear brags a lot.

Your Turn

RETURN TO THE ESSENTIAL QUESTION

 How can stories help you learn a lesson? Talk with a partner. Use the lesson in the story as an example. Ask for more information if you do not understand your partner's ideas.

Classroom Conversation

Now talk about these questions with the class.

1. What do Bear and Brown Squirrel do when they have a problem?

2. What can you tell about each character from how they act when they have a problem?

3. How could Bear and Brown Squirrel each have handled his problem differently?

Response What did you learn from Brown Squirrel about teasing? Write a note to him telling how you feel about teasing. Give text evidence that tells why. Make sure you use complete sentences.

Dear Brown Squirrel,

Writing Tip

When you write a note, include a greeting and a closing. Be sure to add a comma to each.

LACC.2.RL.1.2 recount stories and determine their message, lesson, or moral; **LACC.2.RL.1.3** describe how characters respond to events and challenges; **LACC.2.W.1.1** write opinion pieces; **LACC.2.SL.1.3** ask and answer questions about what a speaker says; **LACC.2.L.1.2.b** use commas in greetings and closings of letters

TRADITIONAL TALES

Why Rabbits
Have Short Tails

☑ GENRE

Traditional tales are stories that have been told for many years.

☑ TEXT FOCUS

The **moral** is the lesson a character learns in a story.

COMMON CORE — **LACC.2.RL.1.2** recount stories and determine their message, lesson, or moral; **LACC.2.RL.4.10** read and comprehend literature

Go Digital

Why Rabbits Have Short Tails

adapted by Gina Sabella

Once Rabbit had a long, beautiful tail. It curled over his back like a furry fan. Rabbit was taking his family on a trip.

"We have to travel in the direction of the stream," Rabbit said. "When we see the hill with the tallest height, we should head toward it."

When they spotted the tallest hill, Rabbit saw that they would have to swim across the stream.

Rabbit liked to brag. He told everyone how clever he was. He did not tell anyone that he could not swim. He did not want anyone to tease him.

Rabbit saw a turtle crawling out of a tunnel. Ten tiny turtles followed behind.

"You have a large family," Rabbit said.

"Yes," Turtle replied. "My family is the biggest in the woods."

"I'm not sure," Rabbit answered. "My family might be bigger."

"Line up your children across the stream," Rabbit said. "Then I can see who has a bigger family." Soon the turtles were lined up. Rabbit and his family jumped on their backs and skipped across the stream.

Turtle was not happy. He tried to grab Rabbit by the tail. But Rabbit's tail snapped off and he hopped away.

Even after it healed, Rabbit's tail never grew long and beautiful again.

Compare Texts

TEXT TO TEXT

Write an Ending Review the moral taught in each of the stories you read. Write a few sentences about which moral you feel is the most important to learn. Explain why.

TEXT TO SELF

Act Out a Lesson The characters in the stories you just read all learn a lesson. Act out for a partner a lesson you have learned. Have your partner guess what you learned.

TEXT TO WORLD

Think About Lessons Think about the lessons taught in each selection. How would things be different in our world if no one learned these lessons? Discuss your ideas with a partner. Build on each other's ideas.

 COMMON CORE **LACC.2.RL.1.2** recount stories and determine their message, lesson, or moral; **LACC.2.SL.1.1.b** build on others' talk in conversations by linking comments to others' remarks

Grammar

Verbs in the Present A **verb** in the **present** names an action that is happening now. Add -*s* or -*es* to this kind of verb when it tells about a singular noun. Do not add -*s* or -*es* when the verb tells about a plural noun.

Verbs After Singular Nouns	Verbs After Plural Nouns
The bear sleeps.	Two bears sleep.
The animal runs.	Many animals run.
The chipmunk rushes.	Some chipmunks rush.

Try This! **Choose the correct verb to complete each sentence. Then write the sentence correctly.**

❶ The squirrel (learn, learns) a lesson.

❷ Bears (scratch, scratches)!

❸ The animal (hide, hides) in a hole.

❹ Days (pass, passes) before the animal comes out.

To make your writing smoother, join two short sentences with the same subject. Write *and* between the two predicates to make one longer sentence. Be sure to use the correct verb forms.

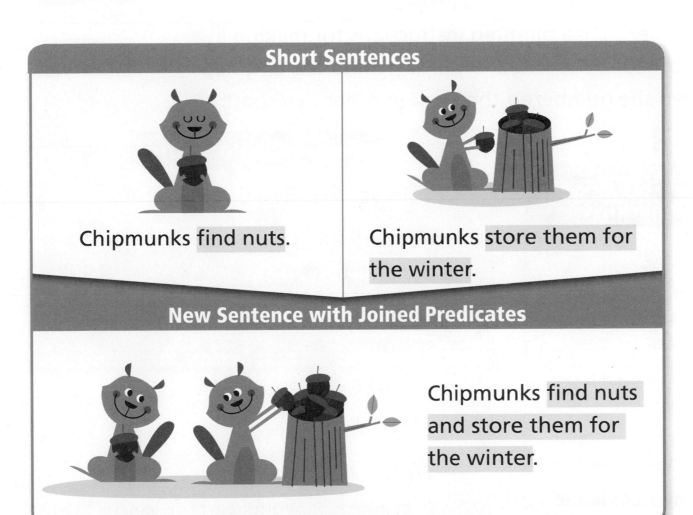

Short Sentences

Chipmunks find nuts.

Chipmunks store them for the winter.

New Sentence with Joined Predicates

Chipmunks find nuts and store them for the winter.

 Connect Grammar to Writing

When you revise your instructions next week, try joining two sentences that have the same subject.

LACC.2.W.1.2 write informative/explanatory texts

Reading-Writing Workshop: Prewriting

Informative Writing

☑ Ideas Before you write **instructions**, think about the important steps. What does your reader need to know to do this project?

When Alexa planned instructions for making a birdfeeder, she listed important materials and steps. Then she numbered the steps in order in a chart.

Writing Process Checklist

▶ **Prewrite**

☑ **Did I think about my audience and purpose?**

☑ **Did I choose a topic I know well?**

☑ **Did I include all the important steps?**

☑ **Are my steps in the correct order?**

Draft

Revise

Edit

Publish and Share

Exploring a Topic

Things You Need

pinecone

peanut butter

birdseed

spoon

∧paper plate

∧string

Steps

2 spread peanut butter on pinecone

4 hang on tree

3 roll in birdseed

1 tie string to pinecone

330

Step Chart

1. Tie a piece of string to a pinecone.

↓

2. Cover the pinecone with peanut butter.

↓

3. Roll the pinecone in birdseed.

↓

4. Hang the birdfeeder in a tree.

Reading as a Writer

What helpful step did Alexa add to her chart? Where can you add important or helpful steps to your own chart?

When I organized my instructions, I made sure I had all the important steps.

Lesson 10

Splash Photography

THE LIFE OF JELLYFISH
Twig C. George

☑ TARGET VOCABULARY

millions

choices

drift

simple

weaker

wrapped

disgusting

decide

Vocabulary
Reader

Coral Reefs

Context
Cards

LACC.2.L.3.6 use words and phrases acquired through conversations, reading and being read to, and responding to texts

Go Digital

Vocabulary in Context

▶ Read each **Context Card**.

▶ Tell a story about two pictures, using the Vocabulary words.

1 **millions**
It looks like this shark has millions of teeth, but it really only has a few dozen.

2 **choices**
Visitors at the aquarium have many choices of things to see.

3 drift

This clever otter will not drift, or float, away.

4 simple

Dolphins make jumping out of the ocean look simple and easy.

5 weaker

One of these crab claws is weaker than the other. It is not very strong.

6 wrapped

The octopus wrapped its strong tentacles around its prey.

7 disgusting

Yuck! The litter around the trash can smells disgusting!

8 decide

Is this a starfish or a crab? You decide.

THE LIFE OF JELLYFISH
Twig C. George

Read and Comprehend

Go Digital

☑ TARGET SKILL

Fact and Opinion A **fact** is something that can be proved true. An **opinion** is a belief or feeling. Authors often include facts and opinions when they write. They also give reasons to support their facts or opinions. The reasons may be in the words or photos of a text.

You can use a chart like this to list facts and opinions.

Fact	Opinion

☑ TARGET STRATEGY

Monitor/Clarify Stop and think when you don't understand something. Find text evidence to help you figure out what doesn't make sense.

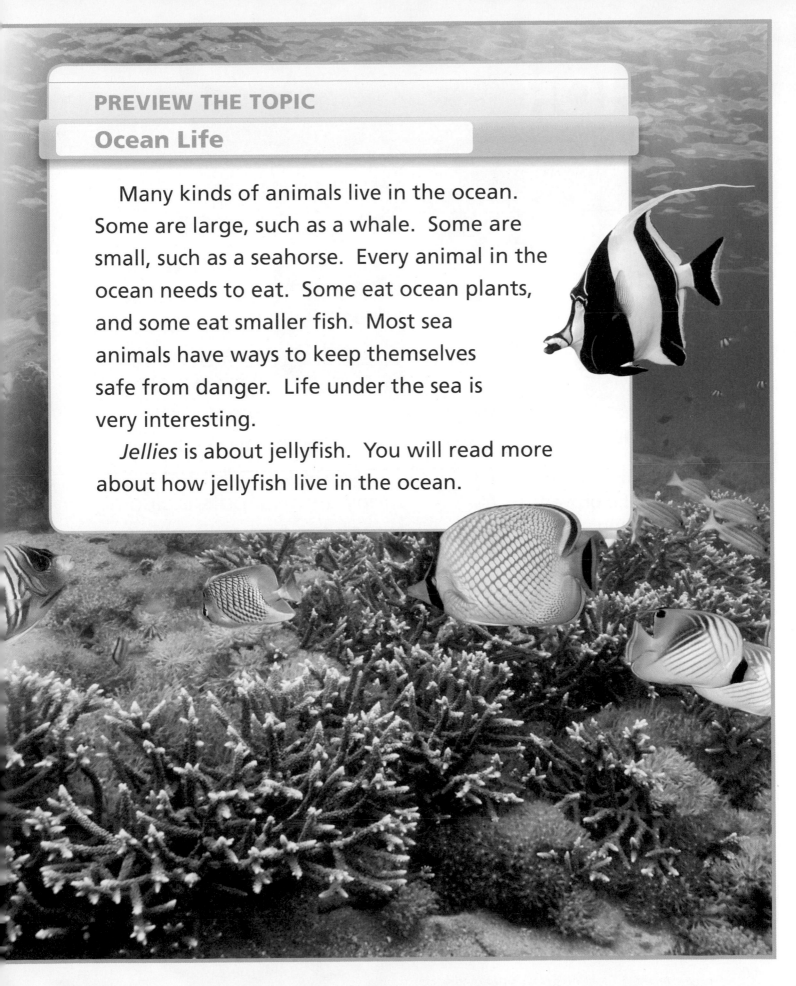

Many kinds of animals live in the ocean. Some are large, such as a whale. Some are small, such as a seahorse. Every animal in the ocean needs to eat. Some eat ocean plants, and some eat smaller fish. Most sea animals have ways to keep themselves safe from danger. Life under the sea is very interesting.

Jellies is about jellyfish. You will read more about how jellyfish live in the ocean.

ANCHOR TEXT

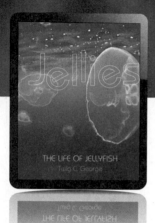

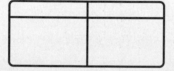

THE LIFE OF JELLYFISH
Twig C. George

☑ TARGET SKILL

Fact and Opinion Tell if an idea can be proved or if it is a feeling.

☑ GENRE

Informational text gives facts about a topic. As you read, look for:

▶ photos and captions
▶ facts and details about a topic

COMMON CORE **LACC.2.RI.2.6** identify the main purpose of a text; **LACC.2.RI.3.8** describe how reasons support points the author makes; **LACC.2.RI.4.10** read and comprehend informational texts

MEET THE AUTHOR

Twig C. George

Twig C. George's love of nature began while she was growing up around her mom, writer Jean Craighead George. The George household had many unusual pets, including tarantulas, sea gulls, crows, and a screech owl that liked to take showers. Twig George raises her own children around nature, too.

Jellies
THE LIFE OF JELLYFISH

by Twig C. George

ESSENTIAL QUESTION

What is special about
animals that live in
the ocean?

If you were a jellyfish you would have two choices—to go up or to go down. That's it. Two. You would not have a brain, so you could not decide what to have for breakfast or where to go for lunch.

Mangrove jellyfish

An unnamed jellyfish

The ocean currents would carry you along from place to place. In this way you could travel hundreds of miles. Food might pass by you and get caught in your tentacles. Or not.

Sea turtles, dolphins, and whale sharks would try to eat you.

You wouldn't worry about it because you couldn't.

You would just float on.

Rhizostone jellyfish

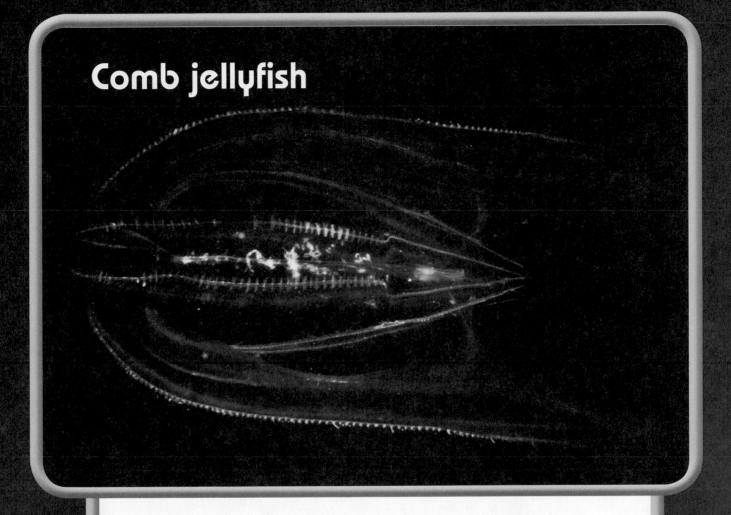

Comb jellyfish

You would protect yourself with millions of tiny, mechanical cells that, when touched by another animal, release a chemical and sting. Like a bow and arrow. You would not know if you were stinging a friend or an enemy. You would not even know what a friend or an enemy was!

Jellyfish sting for protection and to catch food. That's all. They don't hunt and they can't chase. They just bump and sting. Bump and sting.

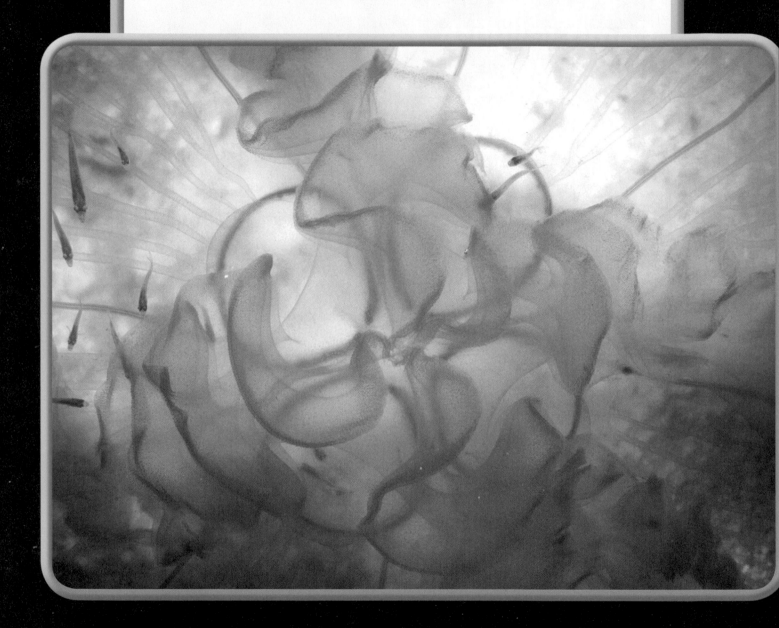

Little fish swim in and out of the dome of this moon jellyfish.

Some jellyfish sting gently. Some jellyfish have a sting so powerful that they are more dangerous than a cobra. These are the Australian box jellies.

Australian
box jellyfish

Thimble jellyfish

Jellyfish are so simple that they look like plastic trash floating in the sea. When an animal eats a jellyfish it stays healthy and strong. When an animal eats plastic it gets weaker and weaker and eventually dies.

Upside-down jellyfish

Some jellyfish lie on the shallow bottom in clear, warm seas and grow their own food. These are called upside-down jellyfish. Once they have eaten small bits of algae, just once, they can grow more inside their bodies by sitting in the sun. They are their own greenhouses and grocery stores all wrapped up in one.

Portuguese man-of-war

To be a jellyfish you need to be shaped like a bell, with at least one mouth, and tentacles. Many animals called jellyfish are really something else. The Portuguese man-of-war is not a real jellyfish. It has an air-filled bubble instead of a water-filled bell.

Jellyfish are almost all water and a little protein. They look slimy and disgusting when they wash up on the beach.

Moon
jellyfish

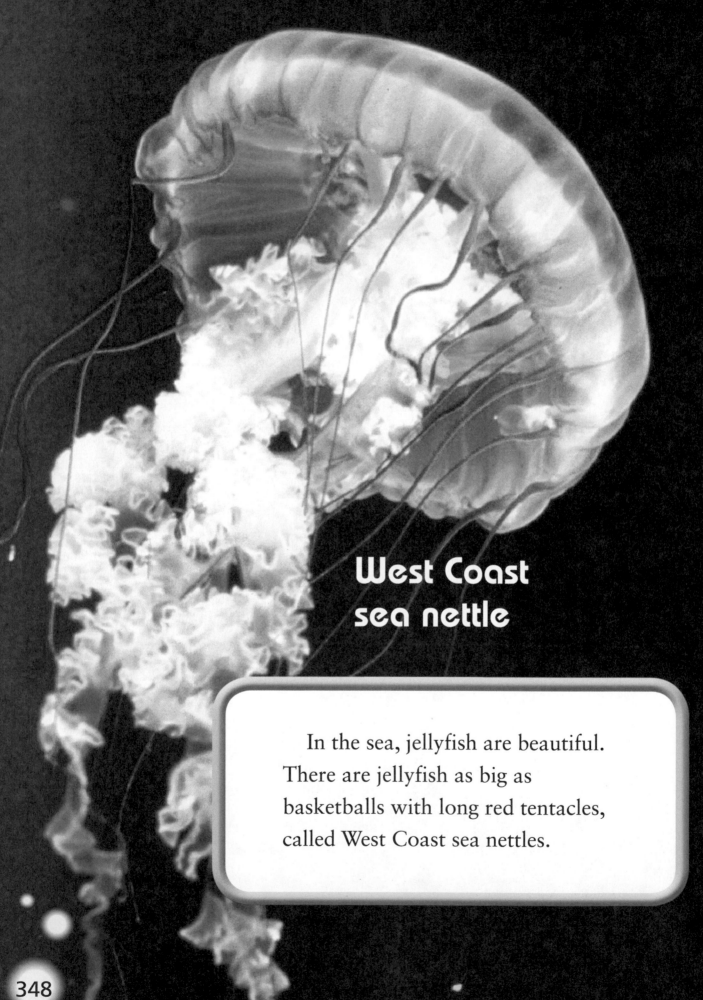

West Coast sea nettle

In the sea, jellyfish are beautiful. There are jellyfish as big as basketballs with long red tentacles, called West Coast sea nettles.

There are tiny, elegant jellyfish that look like a blizzard of snowflakes.

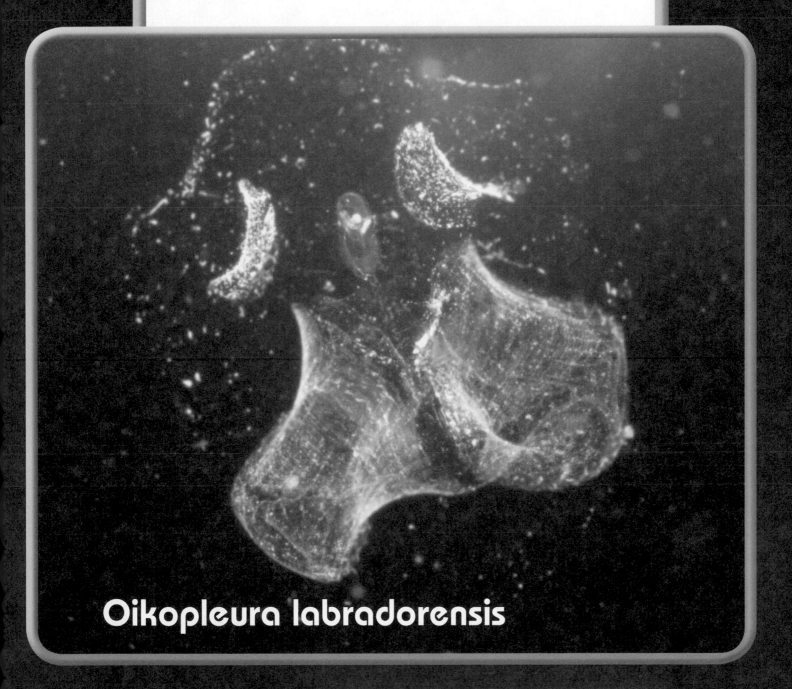

Oikopleura labradorensis

ANALYZE THE TEXT

Fact and Opinion What opinions does the author give? How does the author support those opinions?

Arctic lion's mane jellyfish

There are jellyfish that grow so big that they are as long as a blue whale. They are called Arctic lion's mane jellyfish. They pulse and drift. They eat and reproduce. They live and die. All without a brain or a heart.

Golden Mastigias jellyfish

Someday you might be very lucky and see an ocean full of jellyfish. And, since you have a brain and a heart, you would know you were seeing something unforgettable.

ANALYZE THE TEXT

Author's Purpose What is the author's purpose for writing *Jellies*? How do you know?

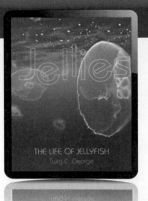

Dig Deeper

Use these pages to learn about Fact and Opinion and Author's Purpose. Then read *Jellies* again. Use what you learn to understand it better.

Fact and Opinion

In *Jellies*, you read facts and opinions about different kinds of jellyfish. A **fact** is something that is true. You can prove a fact. An **opinion** is the way someone feels about something. You cannot prove an opinion. Authors often give reasons to support their facts and opinions.

As you reread, look for facts and opinions. Then find text evidence that supports what the author says. Use a chart to help you keep track of facts and opinions.

Fact	Opinion

LACC.2.RI.2.6 identify the main purpose of a text; **LACC.2.RI.3.8** describe how reasons support points the author makes

Author's Purpose

The reason an author writes a selection is called the **author's purpose.** An author might write to help you learn a lesson. An author might also write to tell facts or to explain an idea. As you reread *Jellies*, think about why the author wrote it.

Your Turn

Turn and Talk

What is special about animals that live in the ocean? Think about what text evidence the author gives to show that jellyfish are special. Share your ideas with a small group. Ask a question if you don't understand a group member's ideas.

Classroom Conversation

Now talk about these questions with the class.

1. What is the author's opinion about jellyfish? What evidence does she give to back it up?

2. How do the photos and captions help you understand more about jellyfish?

3. Using what you learned from the selection, explain what it would be like to be a jellyfish.

WRITE ABOUT READING

Response What do you think about jellyfish? Think about what you learned about jellyfish in *Jellies*. Use text evidence from *Jellies* to give reasons for your opinion. Write a few sentences to tell what you think and why.

Writing Tip

Write your opinion first. Then write two or more reasons for your opinion.

COMMON CORE **LACC.2.RI.3.8** describe how reasons support points the author makes; **LACC.2.W.1.1** write opinion pieces; **LACC.2.SL.1.1.c** ask for clarification and explanation about topics and texts under discussion

INFORMATIONAL TEXT

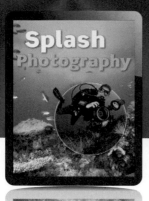

Splash
Photography

☑ GENRE

Informational text gives facts about a topic.

☑ TEXT FOCUS

A **diagram** shows how something works. **Labels** point out important parts of a diagram.

COMMON CORE **LACC.2.RI.2.5** know and use text features to locate facts or information; **LACC.2.RI.3.7** explain how images contribute to and clarify text; **LACC.2.RI.4.10** read and comprehend informational texts

Splash Photography

Smile!

How could you take a picture of a fish swimming under water? You would have to use special equipment, or tools.

People use underwater photography, or taking pictures, for different reasons. A scientist might want to learn more about sharks. Some people like it just because they think it is fun!

Underwater Dress

To take pictures in deep water, a photographer uses a scuba tank, or air tank, to breathe. An underwater photographer also must take lessons to use a scuba tank.

An underwater photographer also wears a mask and swim fins. It is a good idea to wear a rubber suit called a wetsuit. These suits help to keep a person warm and safe from stinging animals.

Using the Right Tools

An underwater photographer uses a special camera to take pictures. The camera is made to keep out water. There are other helpful tools, too. Some tools can be used to light up a dark place. Other tools help to get a closer look at a fish swimming by.

CAMERA

A special camera is used underwater.

SCUBA TANK

This tank holds the air for breathing underwater.

WETSUIT

This suit keeps a photographer safe and warm.

SWIM FINS

A photographer wears fins to swim better.

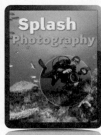

Compare Texts

Compare and Contrast Both selections you read are about the ocean. Think about what you learned in each selection. How are the selections the same? How are they different? Discuss your ideas with a partner.

TEXT TO SELF

Think About Jobs Would you rather write about ocean animals or take pictures of them? Tell why using examples from both selections.

TEXT TO WORLD

Connect to Science Choose an ocean animal that you read about or saw in *Jellies* or *Splash Photography*. Use one or two sources to look up information about the animal. Share your facts with a partner.

Facts About Sharks

LACC.2.RI.3.9 compare and contrast points presented by two texts on same topic; **LACC.2.W.3.7** particpate in shared research and writing projects; **LACC.2.W.3.8** recall information from experiences or gather information to answer a question

Grammar

Verbs in the Present, Past, and Future Some **verbs** name actions that are happening now, or in the **present.** Some verbs name actions that happened before, or in the **past.** Other verbs name actions that will happen later, or in the **future.**

Present	Past	Future
The jellies float.	The jellies floated.	The jellies will float.
We watch them.	We watched them.	We will watch them.

Try This! **Work with a partner. Read the sentences aloud. Tell whether the action is happening in the present, in the past, or in the future.**

❶ I like ocean animals.

❷ Shelley enjoyed the waves.

❸ The jellies swim all around.

❹ We will visit the zoo tomorrow.

362

When you write, make sure your verbs tell about the same time. Your writing will be easier to understand.

Incorrect	Correct
We play at the beach yesterday.	We played at the beach yesterday.
We will jump in the waves yesterday.	We jumped in the waves yesterday.

 Connect Grammar to Writing

When you revise your instructions, be sure all your verbs tell about the same time.

Reading-Writing Workshop: **Revise**

Informative Writing

✔ **Word Choice** It is easier for readers to follow **instructions** if the steps are clear. Choose words that tell your readers exactly what to do.

Alexa wrote instructions for how to make a birdfeeder. Later, Alexa revised her instructions and added exact words.

Writing Process Checklist

Prewrite

Draft

▶ **Revise**

✔ Are my steps in order?

✔ Did I use time-order words, such as *first, next,* and *finally*?

✔ Did I use exact words to make my steps clearer?

✔ Did I tell my readers what to do with what they made?

Edit

Publish and Share

Revised Draft

You can make an easy birdfeeder. You will need a pinecone,

peanut butter, birdseed, a spoon
~~utensil~~, a plate, and string.

First, tie one end of the
the top
string to ~~part~~ of the pinecone.
Cut a long piece of string.

How to Make a Birdfeeder
by Alexa Saperstein

You can make an easy birdfeeder. You will need a pinecone, peanut butter, birdseed, a spoon, a plate, and string.

First, cut a long piece of string. Tie one end of the string to the top of the pinecone. Next, scoop some peanut butter with the spoon, and spread it all over the pinecone. Then, pour some birdseed on the plate. Roll the pinecone in the birdseed. Finally, hang your birdfeeder outside!

Reading as a Writer

Which exact words did Alexa add to make her steps clearer? Where can you add exact words to your own instructions?

I added exact words to make my instructions clearer.

Read "Snow Day" and "Tornado!" As you read, stop and answer each question using text evidence.

Snow Day

It was Friday morning, and Katie was still asleep. Suddenly, she felt her sister jump onto her bed. Katie groaned as she looked at the clock. It was too early to wake up for school.

"Get up!" said Maddie. "You have to see this."

---

1 What clues does the picture give you about when and where this story takes place?

LACC.2.RL.1.1 ask and answer questions to demonstrate understanding of key details; **LACC.2.RL.1.3** describe how characters respond to events or challenges; **LACC.2.RL.2.5** describe the overall structure of a story; **LACC.2.RL.3.7** use information from illustrations and words to demonstrate understanding of characters, setting, or plot; **LACC.2.RL.4.10** read and comprehend literature

Katie got up and looked outside at the front lawn. There was a lot of snow, and it was still snowing! The girls had seen a few snowflakes before, but this was unusual. The whole yard was covered in a blanket of white snow!

"Let's make a snowman before school!" Katie shouted.

They jumped up and ran to their parents' room. "It snowed last night! Can we make a snowman?" they asked.

"Yes," said Mom, "but you have to hurry or you'll be late for the bus!" The girls ran outside and got to work right away building their snowman.

"That's the best snowman I've ever seen!" Mom said after the girls finished. They smiled proudly at their work as they all walked back inside.

---

2 How are Katie's actions different at the beginning of the story than her actions at the middle and the end of the story?

Tornado!

Last summer we had a scary surprise. It was a hot, humid night in June. It looked as if there would be a thunderstorm. Suddenly, the sky turned yellow. Then we heard a strange sound. It sounded like a train.

"A tornado is coming!" my dad said. My whole family ran down to the basement. We pulled an old mattress on top of us to protect us in case anything fell. We could hear the wind blowing and things hitting the house. We were happy when it was over. As we climbed the stairs, we felt anxious because we were about to find out what had happened.

❸ What does the family do when they know the tornado is coming? Do they seem prepared? Use examples from the story to answer.

Our house was fine, but there were branches and leaves everywhere. We had no power in our neighborhood. Our neighbors had lost part of their roof. Dad said calmly, "We have some cleaning up to do, but at least no one was hurt."

❹ How does Dad act at the end of the story? What does this tell you about him?

unit 3

11

CLICK, CLACK, MOO
Cows That Type
by Doreen Cronin pictures by Betsy Lewin

Talk About
Smart
Animals!

✓ TARGET VOCABULARY

understand

gathered

impatient

impossible

believe

problem

demand

furious

Vocabulary
Reader

From
Typewriters
to Computers

Context
Cards

COMMON CORE **LACC.2.L.3.6** use words and phrases acquired through conversations, reading and being read to, and responding to texts

Go Digital

Vocabulary in Context

▶ Read each **Context Card**.

▶ Use a Vocabulary word to tell about something you did.

1 understand

These children talk to each other with their hands. They understand sign language.

2 gathered

The students gathered around the computer in order to see the screen.

3 impatient

This girl looks impatient. She is tired of waiting so long.

4 impossible

It is impossible to hear when there is so much noise.

5 believe

People clap if they believe, or feel, someone has done a good job.

6 problem

Raise your hand if you have a problem or need help.

7 demand

These lights and sirens demand that everyone get out of the way.

8 furious

Babies cry when they are angry. This baby is furious!

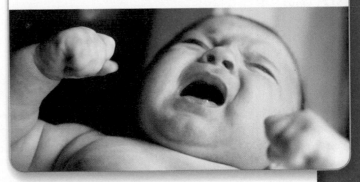

Read and Comprehend

☑ **TARGET SKILL**

Conclusions In *Click, Clack, Moo: Cows That Type*, the author does not tell you everything she wants you to know. You must use story clues from the words and pictures to figure out what the author does not say. This is called **drawing conclusions.** A chart like the one below can be used to list story clues that help you draw conclusions.

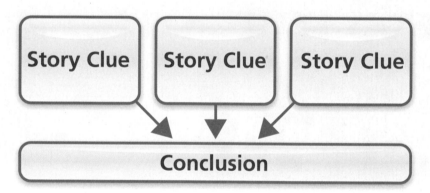

Story Clue   Story Clue   Story Clue

Conclusion

☑ **TARGET STRATEGY**

Infer/Predict Use clues, or text evidence, to figure out more about story parts.

COMMON CORE LACC.2.RL.3.7 use information from illustrations and words to demonstrate understanding of characters, setting, or plot

Animal and Human Interactions

Animals help people do things every day. Some animals are trained to help people do their jobs. Farm animals help by providing things that some people eat and drink. Even pets at home are helpers. They help their owners by keeping them company. *Click, Clack, Moo: Cows That Type* is a story about some farm animals that will not help their farmer.

ANCHOR TEXT

☑ TARGET SKILL

Conclusions Use story clues to figure out more about the text.

☑ GENRE

Humorous fiction is a story that is written to make the reader laugh. As you read, look for:

▶ characters who do or say funny things

▶ events that would not happen in real life

LACC.2.RL.2.4 describe how words and phrases supply rhythm and meaning; **LACC.2.RL.3.7** use information from illustrations and words to demonstrate understanding of characters, setting, or plot; **LACC.2.RL.4.10** read and comprehend literature

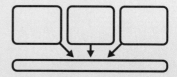

MEET THE AUTHOR

Doreen Cronin

Doreen Cronin's father used to tell her funny stories. Years later, she wrote *Click, Clack, Moo.* Her own story made her laugh, just like her father's had long ago!

MEET THE ILLUSTRATOR

Betsy Lewin

Betsy Lewin's pictures are in many books. She lives in New York with her husband and two cats. She says her cats don't type.

CLICK, CLACK, MOO
Cows That Type

by Doreen Cronin   pictures by Betsy Lewin

ESSENTIAL QUESTION

How can people and animals help each other?

Farmer Brown has a problem.

His cows like to type.

All day long he hears

Click, clack, **moo.**
  Click, clack, **moo.**
Clickety, clack, **moo.**

At first, he couldn't believe his ears.
Cows that type?
Impossible!

Click, clack, **moo.**
  Click, clack, **moo.**
Clickety, clack, **moo.**

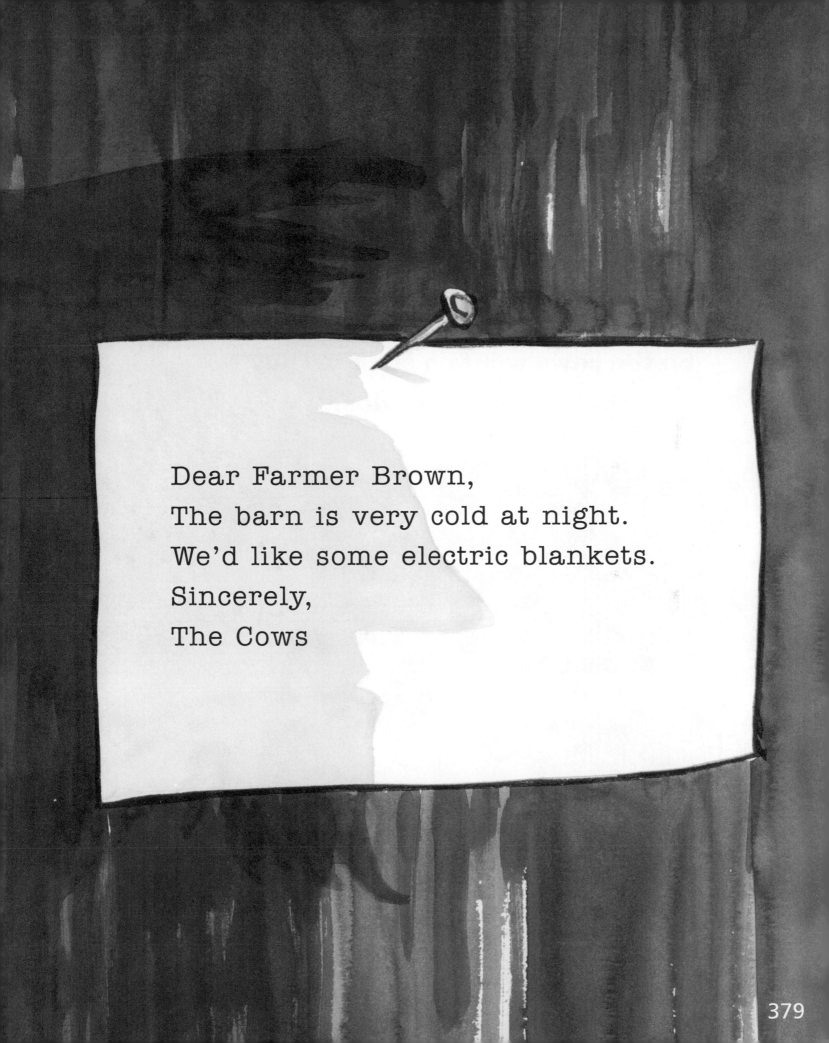

Dear Farmer Brown,
The barn is very cold at night.
We'd like some electric blankets.
Sincerely,
The Cows

It was bad enough the cows had found the old typewriter in the barn, now they wanted electric blankets! "No way," said Farmer Brown. "No electric blankets."

So the cows went on strike. They left a note on the barn door.

Sorry.
We're closed.
No milk today.

"No milk today!" cried Farmer Brown.
In the background, he heard the cows
busy at work:

Click, clack, **moo.**
  Click, clack, **moo.**
Clickety, clack, **moo.**

The next day, he got another note:

Dear Farmer Brown,
The hens are cold too.
They'd like electric blankets.
Sincerely,
The Cows

The cows were growing impatient with the farmer. They left a new note on the barn door.

"No eggs!" cried Farmer Brown. In the background he heard them.

Click, clack, **moo.**
　Click, clack, **moo.**
Clickety, clack, **moo.**

"Cows that type. Hens on strike! Whoever heard of such a thing? How can I run a farm with no milk and no eggs!" Farmer Brown was furious.

ANALYZE THE TEXT

Author's Word Choice "Moo" sounds like the noise a cow makes. What other sound words does the author repeat?

Farmer Brown got out his own typewriter.

Dear Cows and Hens:
There will be no electric blankets.
You are cows and hens.
I demand milk and eggs.
Sincerely,
Farmer Brown

Duck was a neutral party, so he brought the ultimatum to the cows.

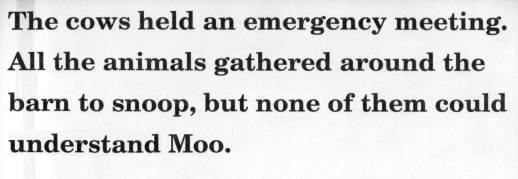

The cows held an emergency meeting. All the animals gathered around the barn to snoop, but none of them could understand Moo.

All night long, Farmer Brown waited for an answer.

Duck knocked on the door early the next morning. He handed Farmer Brown a note:

Dear Farmer Brown,
We will exchange our typewriter
for electric blankets.
Leave them outside the barn door
and we will send Duck over with
the typewriter.
Sincerely,
The Cows

Farmer Brown decided this was a good deal. He left the blankets next to the barn door and waited for Duck to come with the typewriter.

The next morning, he got a note:

Dear Farmer Brown,
The pond is quite boring.
We'd like a diving board.
Sincerely,
The Ducks

Click, clack, **quack.**
  Click, clack, **quack.**
Clickety, clack, **quack.**

Dig Deeper

How to Analyze the Text
Use these pages to learn about Conclusions and Author's Word Choice. Then read *Click, Clack, Moo: Cows That Type* again. Use what you learn to understand it better.

Conclusions

Click, Clack, Moo is a funny story about cows that type. When you read, you need to **draw conclusions** about what the author does not say. For example, on page 376, the author does not tell you the story's setting. You can draw a conclusion from the picture that the story happens on a farm.

Find clues in the words and pictures to help you draw conclusions about the story. Use a chart like the one below.

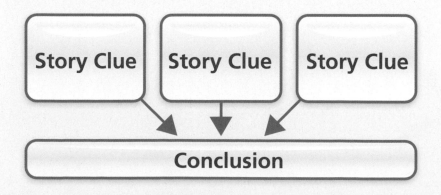

LACC.2.RL.2.4 describe how words and phrases supply rhythm and meaning; LACC.2.RL.3.7 use information from illustrations and words to demonstrate understanding of characters, setting, or plot

Author's Word Choice

Sometimes authors use words that sound like real noises. For example, the cows in *Click, Clack, Moo* use a typewriter. The author writes "Click, clack, moo" to tell what the farmer hears as the cows type. Using words that sound like noises helps the reader imagine what is happening. It makes the story seem more real.

The author repeats these sound words more than once. This **repetition** gives the words in the story a rhythm, or beat.

Your Turn

How can people and animals help each other? Look for text evidence in *Click, Clack, Moo.* Discuss your ideas with a partner. Take turns speaking and listening.

Classroom Conversation

Now talk about these questions with the class.

1 What do the words and illustrations in the story tell you about the characters?

2 Read the last page of the story again. Why doesn't Duck return the typewriter?

3 What do you think other animals on the farm might want from Farmer Brown?

Response How do you think Farmer Brown feels when he gets the note from the ducks? Think about how he responds. Write a few sentences to explain your opinion.

Writing Tip

Remember to use complete sentences when you write your answer. A complete sentence has a subject and a predicate.

Talk About Smart Animals!

Talk About Smart Animals!

☑ GENRE

Informational text gives facts about a topic. This is a magazine article.

☑ TEXT FOCUS

Headings are titles for different parts of a selection.

Talk About Smart Animals!

by Donald Logan

You may think only animals in storybooks or movies do things that seem impossible. You would be wrong!

Meet Rio and Alex. They are real-life animals. Rio is a sea lion. Alex is a parrot. These animals can do things that most people would never believe animals like them could do.

LACC.2.RI.2.5 know and use text features to locate facts or information; **LACC.2.RI.4.10** read and comprehend informational texts

This Sea Lion Can Match

Rio is not like any other sea lion. She can solve a simple problem and tell the answer to her trainers!

Rio has learned to look at three pictures and decide which two are most alike. First, Rio's trainers show her one picture. Rio studies it. Then her trainers add two more pictures. Rio points her nose at the picture that goes best with the first one she saw. When Rio is right, she gets a tasty treat.

Rio is not impatient. She takes her time before she answers.

Rio is deciding which two of these pictures are most alike.

Not Bad for a Bird Brain!

Alex is an African grey parrot. Grey parrots in the wild are often seen gathered together in large groups. In the wild, parrots communicate using bird calls and other sounds. Alex is special because he has learned to talk. He knows over one hundred words!

Alex's owner has also taught Alex to tell colors apart and to count. Alex can even understand questions and answer them.

Sometimes Alex gets tired. He becomes furious and will demand a treat. After a break, he goes right back to solving problems.

"Want a nut!"

Compare Texts

TEXT TO TEXT

Compare Stories Doreen Cronin wrote *Click, Clack, Moo* and *Diary of a Spider* (Lesson 4). With a small group, discuss how the settings and the events of these stories are the same and different.

TEXT TO SELF

Write a Letter Think about the letters that the cows wrote. Write your own letter asking an adult family member for something. Be sure to include commas in your greeting and closing.

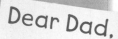

TEXT TO WORLD

Connect to Science With a partner, make a list of things from *Click, Clack, Moo* that the animals in *Talk About Smart Animals!* probably cannot do. Ask and answer questions to make sure you understand what your partner is saying.

COMMON CORE **LACC.2.RL.1.1** ask and answer questions to demonstrate understanding of key details; **LACC.2.SL.1.3** ask and answer questions about what a speaker says; **LACC.2.L.1.2.b** use commas in greetings and closings of letters

Grammar

Compound Sentences A **compound sentence** is made up of two shorter sentences. The shorter sentences are connected by words such as *and, but,* and *or.* Use a comma before the connecting word.

Short Sentences	Compound Sentences
She loves cows. She does not like milking them.	She loves cows, **but** she does not like milking them.
I poured the milk. I finished all of it.	I poured the milk, **and** I finished all of it.
Can you find the farm? Should we ask for directions?	Can you find the farm, **or** should we ask for directions?

Try This! **Write each pair of sentences as a compound sentence. Use a comma and a connecting word.**

❶ The hens lay eggs. We collect them.

❷ Will you eat corn? Do you want potatoes?

❸ I drank milk. Carmen drank juice.

Compound sentences can make your writing less choppy and more interesting. Try joining shorter sentences into compound sentences when you write. This will make your writing smoother.

Short, Choppy Sentences	Compound Sentence
I spent the summer on a farm. I had a great time.	I spent the summer on a farm, and I had a great time.

 Connect Grammar to Writing

When you revise your persuasive letter, try joining shorter sentences into compound sentences.

Opinion Writing

✔️ **Ideas** When you write a letter to persuade, be sure your opinion and goal are clear to your reader. Give reasons to explain your opinion using linking words such as *because* and *also*.

Kurt drafted a **persuasive letter.** Later, he revised it to clearly say his reason for writing. Use the Writing Traits Checklist to revise your writing.

Writing Traits Checklist

✔️ **Ideas**
Did I state my goal clearly?

✔️ **Organization**
Did I use the parts of a letter? Did I use linking words to connect my reasons to my opinion?

✔️ **Voice**
Does my writing tell how I feel?

✔️ **Conventions**
Did I use commas correctly in the greeting and closing?

Revised Draft

Dear Auntie Lorrie,

I'm writing to ask you ~~for~~ to send me some of your old children's books. ~~something.~~ It's for a really

good cause because some

of the books in our classroom

are falling apart.

Kurt Atchley
244 Austin St.
Ojai, CA 93023
January 24, 2014

Dear Auntie Lorrie,

   I'm writing to ask you to send me some of your old children's books. It's for a really good cause because some of the books in our classroom are falling apart. Also, we have no money for new books. Can you help us? I hope so.

                                            Love,
                                            Kurt

Reading as a Writer

What did Kurt do to make his goal clearer? What reasons and linking words did he use? How can you make your goal clearer?

I made sure my goal was stated clearly.

Ah, Music!

Written and illustrated by Aliki

THERE'S A HOLE AT THE Bottom OF THE Sea

✅ TARGET VOCABULARY

vibration

tune

volume

expression

creative

performance

concentrate

relieved

Vocabulary Reader

Bongos, Maracas, and Xylophones

Context Cards

COMMON CORE

LACC.2.L.3.6 use words and phrases acquired through conversations, reading and being read to, and responding to texts

Vocabulary in Context

▶ Read each **Context Card**.

▶ Make up a new sentence that uses a Vocabulary word.

1

vibration

The drummer feels the vibration of the drums and cymbals when he hits them.

2

tune

He played the same tune over and over again as he learned the new song.

3 volume

The girl didn't hear her mom because the volume of the music was too loud.

4 expression

The voices of the singers were so powerful and had so much expression!

5 creative

Our music teacher told us to be creative, so we made up a new song to play.

6 performance

The musicians played their best during the performance on the stage.

7 concentrate

The girl is focusing on the music. She has to concentrate to learn it.

8 relieved

The conductor was relieved that the musicians played the music correctly.

Written and Illustrated by *Aliki*

Read and Comprehend

✓ **TARGET SKILL**

Text and Graphic Features Authors sometimes include special features when they write. These are called **text and graphic features.** Pictures, headings, and captions are examples of text and graphic features. These can help you understand the text. They can also help you find information in the text.

Use this chart to list text and graphic features and tell how they help you.

Text or Graphic Feature	Page Number	Purpose

✓ **TARGET STRATEGY**

Question Ask questions about what you are reading. Answer using text evidence.

 LACC.2.RI.2.5 know and use text features to locate facts or information; **LACC.2.RI.3.7** explain how images contribute to and clarify text

408

Music can be made in many ways. You can play an instrument, such as a piano or a flute. You can make your own instruments, too. For example, you can hit a can with a spoon to make a drum. Your voice can even be like an instrument. You can whistle, hum, or sing to make music. You can make music almost anywhere. You will read more about music in *Ah, Music!*

ANCHOR TEXT

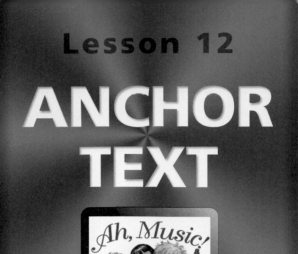

Ah, Music!

☑ TARGET SKILL

Text and Graphic Features Tell how words and pictures help you understand new information.

☑ GENRE

Informational text gives facts about a topic. As you read, look for:

▸ pictures and captions
▸ information about the real world

 LACC.2.RI.2.5 know and use text features to locate facts or information; **LACC.2.RI.3.7** explain how images contribute to and clarify text; **LACC.2.RI.3.8** describe how reasons support points the author makes; **LACC.2.RI.4.10** read and comprehend informational texts

MEET THE AUTHOR AND ILLUSTRATOR

Aliki

Ever since she was a young girl, Aliki has been writing down her feelings. She thinks that doing this was good practice for when she became an author. *Ah, Music!* took over three years for Aliki to write and draw. She had to do a lot of studying to find out about music and what different instruments looked like.

Ah, Music!

written and illustrated by Aliki

ESSENTIAL QUESTION

What are different ways
to enjoy music?

411

Music Is Sound

If you hum a tune,

play an instrument,

or clap out a rhythm,

you are making music.
You are listening to it, too.

Music Is Rhythm

That is the beat I can clap.

Rhythm is a marching-band beat, a puffing-train beat,

a beating-the-eggs beat, a heart beat.
Some rhythm beats are stronger than others.
You can count the accents.

A person who cannot hear
can feel the vibration of the beat.

Music Is Melody

That is the tune I can hum,

or the song that is sung
if words are set to music.
Often the words are poetry.

Twinkle, Twinkle,
little star,
How I wonder
what you are.
Up above the world
so high,
Like a diamond
in the sky . . .

I didn't know
you could sing.

Music Is Volume

That is the loudness or the softness of the sound.

Shhh.

ANALYZE THE TEXT

Text and Graphic Features What is the heading on this page? How do the illustrations help you understand the heading and the text?

415

Music Is Feeling

It sets a mood.

Music speaks not with words, as in a song.
It speaks with expression.
Everyone can understand music, because everyone has feelings.
Music can make you feel happy or sad or scared.
It can make you want to dance, to march, to sing,
or to be quiet, to listen, and to dream.

*Here will we sit
and let the sounds of music
creep in our ears.*

Shakespeare said that.

I listen to music,
and I can see pictures
in my head.

I imagine I hear
twittering birds.

I hear a cool waterfall.

I see a brilliant sunrise.

I see a scary dark forest.

I hear a noisy city.

Music Is a Creative Art

Just as a writer uses words,

or an artist uses paint,

a composer uses music
to create images and feelings.
He or she writes it down in notes, symbols,
and numbers on lines and spaces.
The notations describe the rhythm, tone, pitch,
feeling, and even the silences of the piece.

Practice Makes Perfect

We make music.
Making music is hard fun.
It takes lots of practice to learn to
play an instrument.

But when you do, it is forever.

That's the hard part.

Here's the fun part.

As you practice and learn,
you begin to make
beautiful sounds.
Practice becomes fun.

You learn new pieces to play.
You feel proud.
Your music teacher says
you will play in a recital.
You will play for an audience.

*A metronome
helps keep time.*

ANALYZE THE TEXT

Fact and Opinion What is the author's opinion about practicing music? What reasons support the author's opinion?

The Performance

She must be nervous.

At your recital it is your turn to play.
Everyone is looking at you.

You concentrate.
You do the best you can.

When you finish, everyone claps.
It sounds like waves breaking.
It feels good. You take a bow.
You feel relieved and very proud.

You celebrate.
Everyone says you did well.
Next time it will be even
better, because you are
learning more every day.
Practice makes perfect.

Music Is for Everybody

Dig Deeper

How to Analyze the Text

Use these pages to learn about Text and Graphic Features and Fact and Opinion. Then read *Ah, Music!* again. Use what you learn to understand it better.

Text and Graphic Features

In *Ah, Music!*, you read about music. The headings, pictures, and other **text and graphic features** help you understand more about what you read. Headings tell you what each section is about. Pictures give you more information about the text.

Use a chart like the one below to list the text and graphic features. Also list each feature's purpose, or how it helps you.

Text or Graphic Feature	Page Number	Purpose

LACC.2.RI.2.5 know and use text features to locate facts or information; **LACC.2.RI.3.7** explain how images contribute to and clarify text; **LACC.2.RI.3.8** describe how reasons support points the author makes

Fact and Opinion

Authors of informational texts often give both facts and opinions. A **fact** is something that can be proved true or false. An **opinion** is what someone believes or feels. When you read a selection, look for facts and opinions. Also look for the reasons the author gives to support a fact or an opinion.

Your Turn

 What are different ways to enjoy music? Talk with a partner about your ideas. Use text evidence, such as the headings and pictures in *Ah, Music!*, to help you answer.

Classroom Conversation

Now talk about these questions with the class.

1. What words does the author use to describe and tell about rhythm? Use the headings to help you find this information.

2. Why is it important to practice when learning to play an instrument?

3. Why did the author write this selection?

Response Look back at page 416. How does the author say that music can make you feel? Do you agree? Write a few sentences to tell why or why not. Use the pictures and words that the author uses to help you.

Writing Tip

Break sentences that are too long into two shorter sentences.

COMMON CORE LACC.2.RI.1.1 ask and answer questions to demonstrate understanding of key details; LACC.2.RI.2.5 know and use text features to locate facts or information; LACC.2.RI.2.6 identify the main purpose of a text; LACC.2.RI.3.7 explain how images contribute to and clarify text; LACC.2.W.1.1 write opinion pieces

SONG

THERE'S A HOLE
AT THE
Bottom
OF THE
Sea

THERE'S A HOLE AT THE Bottom OF THE Sea

A song is like a poem that is set to
music. A song has a rhythm, or a beat.
Some songs also rhyme and have repeated
words, just like some poems do.

Each section of a song is called a verse.
The song you will read has several verses.
Each verse has repeated words from the
earlier verses. After you read the words,
try singing the song!

1. There's a hole at the bot-tom of the sea

There's a hole at the bot-tom of the sea,

There's a hole, There's a hole,

There's a hole at the bot-tom of the sea.

2. There's a log in the hole at the bottom of the sea,
   There's a log in the hole at the bottom of the sea,
   There's a log, there's a log,
   There's a log in the hole at the bottom of the sea.

3. There's a bump on the log in the hole
   at the bottom of the sea,
   There's a bump on the log in the hole
   at the bottom of the sea,
   There's a bump, there's a bump
   There's a bump on the log in the hole
   at the bottom of the sea.

4. There's a frog on the bump on the log in the hole
   at the bottom of the sea…

5. There's a tail on the frog on the bump on the log
   in the hole at the bottom of the sea…

6. There's a speck on the tail on the frog on the bump
   on the log in the hole at the bottom of the sea…

Compare Texts

TEXT TO TEXT

Compare Rhythm How are *Ah, Music!* and *There's a Hole at the Bottom of the Sea* alike? How are they different? Think about how the authors use words and rhythm in each selection.

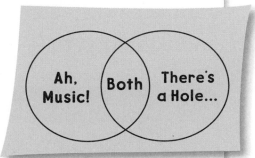

Ah, Music! | Both | There's a Hole...

TEXT TO SELF

Describe an Instrument What instrument would you like to play at a recital? Why? Share your ideas with a partner.

TEXT TO WORLD

Using Text Features What features in *Ah, Music!* can you also find in other informational books? How do those features help you find and understand information easily?

COMMON CORE **LACC.2.RL.2.4** describe how words and phrases supply rhythm and meaning; **LACC.2.RI.2.5** know and use text features to locate facts or information

Grammar

Compound Sentences A **compound sentence** is two **simple sentences** joined by a comma and the word *and, but,* or *or.* You can make **compound sentences** more interesting by moving words around and adding details.

Compound Sentence	Improved Compound Sentence
I listen to music, and I see pictures in my head.	I listen to music, and I see beautiful pictures in my head.
Writers use words, but composers use notes.	Words are used by writers, but composers use musical notes.

Try This! **Move words around or add details to make each compound sentence more interesting.**

❶ I listen to music, and I feel happy.

❷ People use music for fun, and music can help people relax.

❸ The violin is hard to play, but I like playing the piano.

When you write, you can join short, choppy sentences to make one longer sentence. You can also move words around and add details. This makes your writing more interesting.

Short, Choppy Sentences

Lupe plays the tuba.

Her brother Jaime plays the flute.

Longer, More Interesting Sentence

Lupe plays the tuba very well, and her brother Jaime is a good flute player.

 ## Connect Grammar to Writing

When you revise your opinion paragraph, look for short sentences that you can combine. Combine them with a comma and the word *and, but,* or *or*.

Opinion Writing

☑ **Voice** When you write to persuade, share your opinion in the introduction sentence. Use linking words such as *and, because,* and *also* to connect opinions and reasons. Tell your opinion again in the closing sentence.

Han wrote an **opinion paragraph** about music. Later he added words to clearly tell how he feels. He also added linking words.

Writing Traits Checklist

☑ **Ideas**
Did I use linking words to connect opinions and reasons?

☑ **Organization**
Did I state my opinion at the beginning and end of my paragraph?

☑ **Voice**
Does my writing show how I feel about my subject?

☑ **Sentence Fluency**
Did I vary the length of my sentences?

Revised Draft

love
I ~~like~~ music. Music has something
, and people all over the world
for everyone. enjoy music
          also   because it
Music is powerful. ~~It~~ can make

you feel happy, sad, or even

scared.

Music for Everyone
by Han Choi

I love music. Music has something for everyone, and people all over the world enjoy music. Music is also powerful because it can make you feel happy, sad, or even scared. There are many ways to enjoy music. You can sing, dance, play an instrument, or just listen. All children should have a chance to make music.

Reading as a Writer

What did Han add to let you know how he feels about his subject? What can you add to your writing to let your reader know how you feel?

I added sentences to show how I feel about my subject.

Lesson 13

Around the World
Schools

An American School

✓ TARGET VOCABULARY

culture

community

languages

transportation

subjects

lessons

special

wear

Vocabulary Reader

One Room Schools

Context Cards

COMMON CORE **LACC.2.L.3.6** use words and phrases acquired through conversations, reading and being read to, and responding to texts

Go Digital

Vocabulary in Context

▶ Read each **Context Card**.

▶ Talk about a picture. Use a different Vocabulary word from the one on the card.

1 **culture**

Culture is the traditions and beliefs of a group of people.

2 **community**

A community is a group of people who live together in a certain area.

3 languages

People use different languages to write and to speak to one another.

4 transportation

People use transportation to get from one place to another.

5 subjects

Science is one of the subjects taught in school.

6 lessons

This teacher gives lessons to his students. The students learn from each lesson.

7 special

These students go to a special school for music. They play music every day.

8 wear

These two students wear uniforms at school.

Read and Comprehend

Go Digital

Main Idea and Details The **topic** of an informational text is what the selection is about. The **main idea** is the most important idea about the topic. **Details** tell more about the main idea. You can show a main idea on a chart like this. List the details that make the main idea clearer.

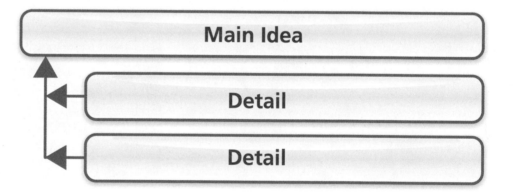

Main Idea
Detail
Detail

☑ **TARGET STRATEGY**

Analyze/Evaluate To **analyze** as you read, think about the author's words and the photos. Then **evaluate**, or decide, how the words and photos help you know what is important in the selection.

COMMON CORE **LACC.2.RI.1.2** identify the main topic of a multiparagraph text and the focus of specific paragraphs; **LACC.2.RI.3.7** explain how images contribute to and clarify text

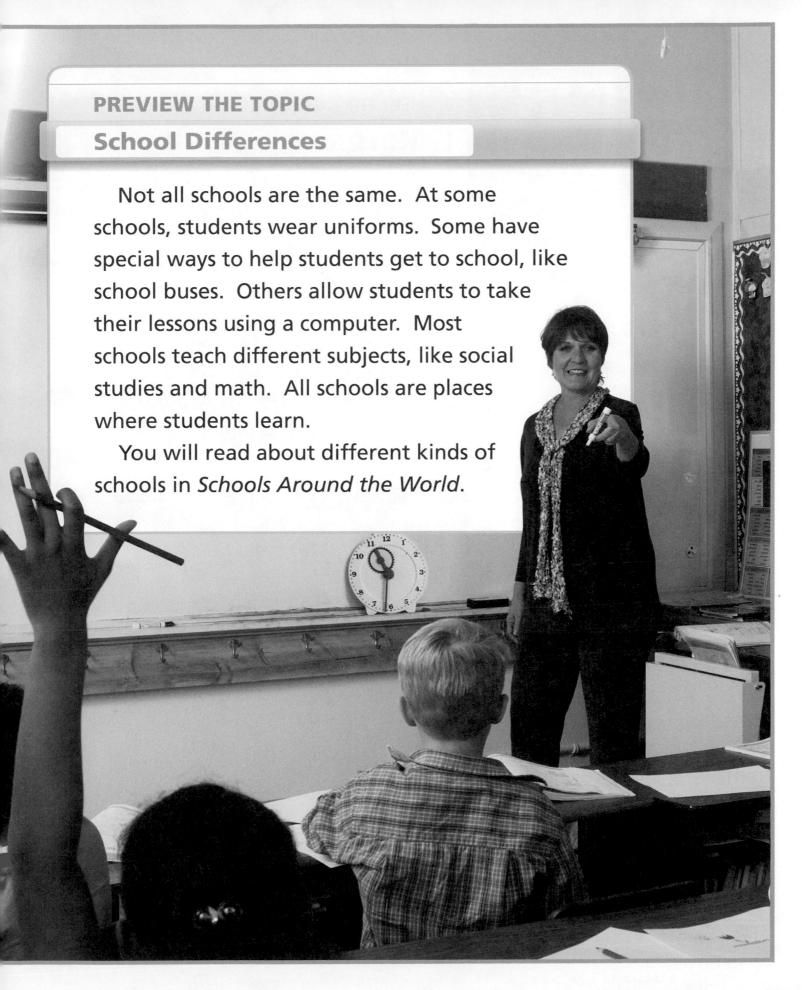

School Differences

Not all schools are the same. At some schools, students wear uniforms. Some have special ways to help students get to school, like school buses. Others allow students to take their lessons using a computer. Most schools teach different subjects, like social studies and math. All schools are places where students learn.

You will read about different kinds of schools in *Schools Around the World*.

ANCHOR TEXT

Around the World
Schools

Main Idea and Details Tell important ideas and details about a topic.

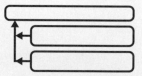

Informational text gives facts about a topic. As you read, look for:

▶ photos and captions
▶ facts and details about a topic

MEET THE AUTHOR

Margaret C. Hall

Margaret C. Hall has written many nonfiction books for children. Her books include topics ranging from national parks to mallard ducks. *Schools Around the World* is part of a series of books she wrote. Other books in the series include *Homes Around the World* and *Games Around the World*.

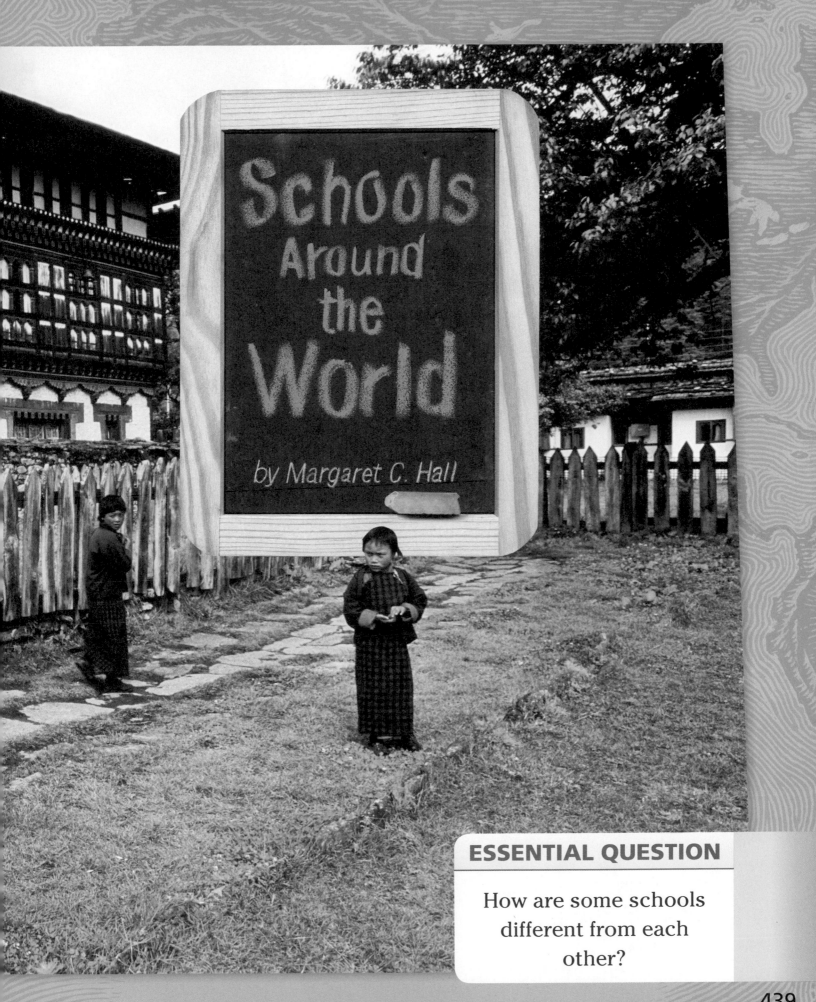

Schools
Around
the
World

by Margaret C. Hall

Schools Around the World

All around the world, children go to school.
Some children spend most of their day at school.
Others spend only a few hours there.

Some school buildings in Asia are tall, like this one.

440

These students in an American classroom start their day by saying the Pledge of Allegiance.

Schools are different in different parts of the world. But they are all the same in one way. Schools are where children go to learn.

AMAZING SCHOOL FACTS

A long time ago, a German man started a new kind of school. He thought that small children should grow like flowers in a garden. He called his school kindergarten. The word means "children's garden" in German.

These students in Tibet, China, are about to start their morning classes.

School Buildings

The kind of school buildings children have depends on where they live. It depends on the climate and the resources of their community.

School buildings can be large or small. They can be made from many different materials. Some children even go to school outside or in buildings with no walls.

🔔 **AMAZING SCHOOL FACTS**

Schools have been around for thousands of years. The first schools were started to teach children about their culture.

Getting to School

Children travel to school in many different ways. The kind of transportation they use depends on where they live. It also depends on how far they have to go.

Many children walk or ride bicycles to school. Others ride in cars, on buses, or on a train. Some children go to school by boat.

AMAZING SCHOOL FACTS

In some places, children live too far away from their school to go there. Teachers give lessons over the radio or by using computers that are hooked up to the school.

School Clothing

Children around the world wear different kinds of clothing to school. What they wear often depends on the climate where they live. It also depends on what season it is.

In some schools, the students all dress alike. They wear uniforms. Students from different schools have different uniforms.

▲ *Students at this girls' school in Panama wear blue skirts and sweaters as part of their uniforms.*

These students in Germany are learning science on a class trip with their teachers.

The School Day

All around the world, teachers help students learn new things. Children do some schoolwork in groups. They do other schoolwork on their own.

Most children eat lunch or a snack at school. They may also have time to play. At many schools, children take class trips, too.

This teacher answers a question for his student at a school in Cuba.

Learning to Read and Write

One important job for teachers is to help children learn to read and write. Students learn to read and write in many different languages. The language children use at school depends on where they live. Some children study their own language and another language, too.

ANALYZE THE TEXT

Text and Graphic Features How do the photos and captions help you understand more about the schools?

At an American school overseas, students study a map of Europe.

Other Lessons

Children learn many things at school. All around the world, they study math and science. They learn about their own country and other countries, too.

Many children around the world study art and music in school. They may also learn how to use a computer.

These students in Great Britain practice playing music at school.

In this school in Japan, students help serve lunch.

School Chores

Most children have chores to do at school. They help to keep the classroom neat and clean. They may even help to set up the classroom every day.

In some places, children work to keep the schoolyard neat and clean. Some children may serve lunch to one another.

This teacher gives extra help to students after school.

After School

Some children go to school even after the school day is over. They may have a tutor to help them with the subjects that are harder for them.

Some children have other lessons after school. They study things they cannot learn in school. They may learn about dance, music, or their own culture.

These boys in Israel learn about their culture.

449

Students at this boarding school eat, study, and live together.

Special Schools

Some children live at their schools. These schools are called boarding schools. The children go home for visits and on holidays.

This girl cannot see. She goes to a school where she can learn to read and write in a special way. People who are blind read with their fingers. They use a system of raised dots called Braille.

Home Schooling

A home can also be a school. Some parents teach their children at home. They want to decide exactly what their children will learn.

People at schools will often help parents plan home lessons for their children. Many children who study at home go to a school for gym or art classes.

This mother is teaching her daughter at home.

School and Work

Some children work as performers. They spend part of their day practicing the work that they do. They spend the rest of the day studying regular school subjects.

The students below perform a traditional Russian dance.

452

One of the subjects that was taught in ancient Greece was gymnastics. The ancient Greeks thought gymnastics was just as important to learn as math or reading!

This boy is learning gymnastics.

Older Students

Many people go to school even after they are adults. They may go to college. Or, they may go to a trade school to learn how to do a certain job.

Adults also take classes for fun. They study different languages and learn how to do things. No matter how old students are, they go to school to learn.

ANALYZE THE TEXT

Main Idea and Details What is the topic of *Schools Around the World*? How does the main idea of the section "Older Students" fit with the topic?

These women in India go to school at night.

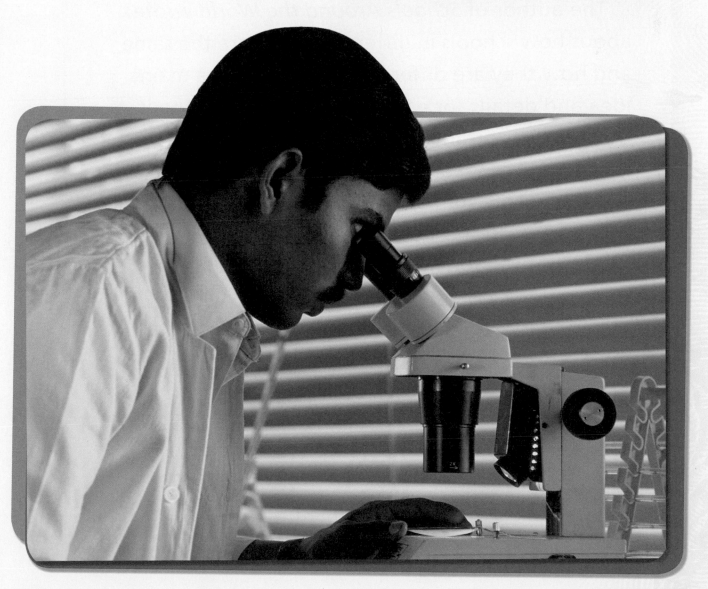

Dig Deeper

How to Analyze the Text

Use these pages to learn about Main Idea and Details and Text and Graphic Features. Then read *Schools Around the World* again. Use what you learn to understand it better.

Main Idea and Details

The author of *Schools Around the World* wrote about how schools in different places are the same and how they are different. She included a main idea and details for each section. A **main idea** is the most important idea in the section. The **details** tell more about the main idea.

As you read, think about the main idea and details of each section. Use this chart to record a main idea and the details that tell about it.

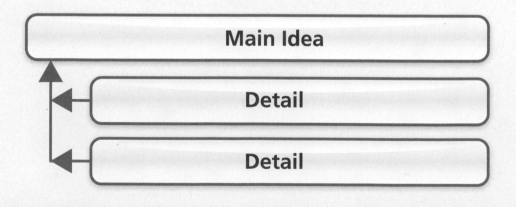

LACC.2.RI.1.2 identify the main topic of a multiparagraph text and the focus of specific paragraphs; **LACC.2.RI.2.5** know and use text features to locate facts or information; **LACC.2.RI.3.7** explain how images contribute to and clarify text

Text and Graphic Features

Authors often use **text and graphic features** to help make their writing clear. Headings, captions, and photos are some text and graphic features in *Schools Around the World*.

Text and graphic features can help you understand the text. They can also help you find information quickly. For example, headings tell what each section is about. As you read, think about and use the text and graphic features.

Your Turn

How are some schools different from each other? Use text evidence from *Schools Around the World* to help you answer. Discuss your ideas with a partner. Take turns talking.

Classroom Conversation

Now talk about these questions with the class.

1 How do the headings help you figure out the main idea of each section?

2 Why do you think the author wrote *Schools Around the World*? How do you know?

3 How do some children get to school? Use the headings to look back and find the answer.

WRITE ABOUT READING

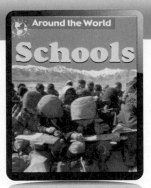

Response Look back through *Schools Around the World.* Find facts that are interesting to you. Then write sentences that tell two ways that schools are alike and two ways that schools are different. Draw pictures to go with your sentences.

All schools help people learn.

Writing Tip

Make sure that each statement ends with a period.

Go Digital

COMMON CORE **LACC.2.RI.1.2** identify the main topic of a multiparagraph text and the focus of specific paragraphs; **LACC.2.RI.2.5** know and use text features to locate facts or information; **LACC.2.RI.2.6** identify the main purpose of a text; **LACC.2.W.1.2** write informative/explanatory texts; **LACC.2.SL.1.1.a** follow rules for discussions

INFORMATIONAL TEXT

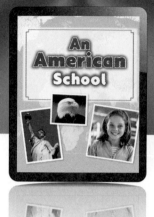

An American School

An American School

Hi, my name is Lily. I go to Washington Elementary School. Aki is my pen pal from Japan. She came for a visit. She wants to ask me some questions about my school.

Aki

Lily

Go Digital

Aki: How did your school get its name?

Lily: My school is named after George Washington who was the first president of the United States. The president is the main leader of our country. The president represents our nation around the world. Our president lives and works in a special home called the White House in Washington, D.C.

Aki: How do you start your day at school?

Lily: We start our day with a pledge to our flag. This is how we honor, or respect, our country and its people. Our flag is red, white, and blue and has stars and stripes. There are fifty stars, and each one stands for one of the fifty states in the United States.

Aki: What subjects do you learn about in school?

Lily: We learn about math and science. We also read a lot of books and learn new words. My favorite subject is social studies.

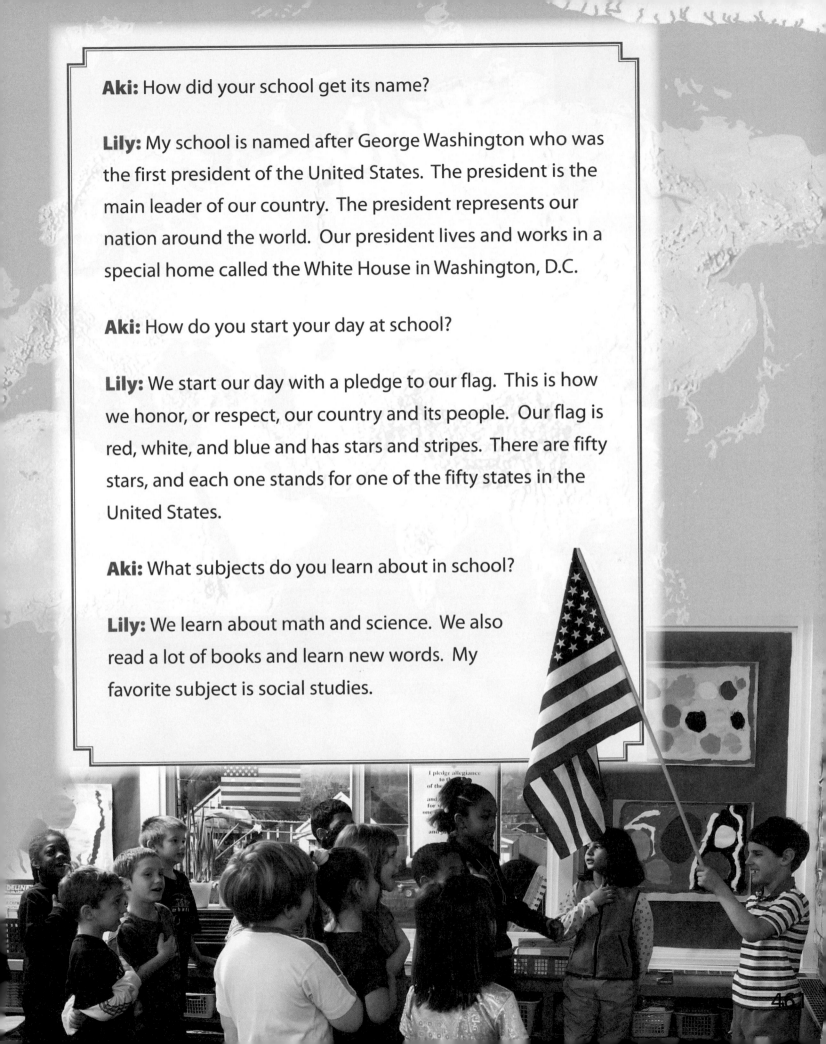

Aki: What are you learning about in social studies?

Lily: This week we are learning about symbols of the United States, like our flag. Our teacher said that the bald eagle is another symbol. It represents a strong and free country. The Statue of Liberty is also a symbol. When people see it, they think of hope and freedom.

Aki: What are some fun things you do at school?

Lily: I like our music class because we get to sing our favorite songs and play musical instruments. This week we played drums and bells. I also like going to check out books at our school library!

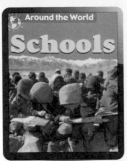

Compare Texts

TEXT TO TEXT

Write Interview Questions What questions would you ask a school principal? Think about *Schools Around the World* and *An American School*. Use both selections to help you think of questions. Make a list of what you would ask.

TEXT TO SELF

Draw and Label What type of school from *Schools Around the World* would you like to go to? Draw what the school might look like. Write labels to tell about your picture.

TEXT TO WORLD

Connect to Social Studies With a small group, choose one of the countries you read about in *Schools Around the World*. Use books and other sources to read about schools in that country. Make a poster that shows what you learned.

Schools in Germany

Go Digital

COMMON CORE LACC.2.RI.1.1 ask and answer questions to demonstrate understanding of key details; LACC.2.RI.3.9 compare and contrast points presented by two texts on the same topic; LACC.2.W.3.7 participate in shared research and writing projects

Grammar

 Go Digital

Quotation Marks When you write, show what someone says by putting **quotation marks** (" ") at the beginning and end of the speaker's exact words.

Rules for Using Quotation Marks

Put a **comma** after words such as *said* and *asked*.

> The teacher said, "Take out your math books."

Begin the first word inside the quotation marks with a **capital letter**.

> Mike said, "We are having a quiz today."

Put the **end mark** inside the quotation marks.

> Liza asked, "Who is the class leader?"

Try This! **Write each sentence correctly. Include quotation marks to show the exact words someone said or asked.**

1. The bus driver said stay in your seats.

2. Jack asked how long is the trip?

3. The teacher said it will take an hour.

You have read stories in which people talk to each other. This makes a story more interesting. Make your own writing more interesting by showing the words people speak.

Quotation Marks

Nita asked, "What is your favorite subject in school?"
Raj said, "My favorite subject is science."

 ## Connect Grammar to Writing

When you edit your persuasive paragraph, be sure to use commas, capital letters, and end marks correctly.

COMMON CORE LACC.2.W.1.1 write opinion pieces; LACC.2.L.3.5.b distinguish shades of meaning among verbs and adjectives

Opinion Writing

✓ **Word Choice** When you write to persuade, use exact words to make your writing more interesting.

Rachel wrote a **persuasive paragraph** asking her teacher to take her class to a museum. Later, she revised her writing to use more exact words. Use exact words when you revise your paragraph.

Writing Traits Checklist

✓ **Organization**
Did I state my opinion at the beginning?

✓ **Word Choice**
Did I use exact words to make my writing interesting?

✓ **Voice**
Did I choose reasons that are important to my audience?

✓ **Sentence Fluency**
Did I begin my sentences in different ways?

Revised Draft

Our class should go to the Children's Museum.

The Children's Museum has many wonderful ~~lots of nice~~ displays, such as one that shows important people from the past. That's a great display because we're learning about that in social studies right now.

466

Let's Take a Trip!

by Rachel Wollmer

Our class should go to the Children's Museum. The Children's Museum has many wonderful displays, such as one that shows important people from the past. That's a great display because we're learning about that in social studies right now. Also, we could write a research paper about what we learn at the museum. Everyone would have a fun day together at the Children's Museum!

Reading as a Writer

Which exact words did Rachel add? What words can you add to make your writing more interesting?

I used exact words to make my writing interesting to my readers.

Helen Keller
by Jane Sutcliffe · Illustrations by Elaine Verstraete

Talking TOOLS

☑ TARGET VOCABULARY

knowledge

curious

motion

silence

illness

imitated

darkness

behavior

Vocabulary Reader

Context Cards

LACC.2.L.3.6 use words and phrases acquired through conversations, reading and being read to, and responding to texts

Vocabulary
in Context

▶ Read each **Context Card**.

▶ Ask a partner a question that uses one of the Vocabulary words.

1 **knowledge**

Knowledge, or information, can come from books and many other places.

2 **curious**

You can search the Internet if you are curious, or want to learn, about sea animals.

3 motion

A hand held up is a **motion** to stop!

4 silence

The rule in the library is "**Silence!** Please don't speak."

5 illness

This child has an **illness**, but she won't be sick for long.

6 imitated

This girl **imitated**, or copied, her teacher to learn sign language.

7 darkness

Flashlights help people see better in **darkness**.

8 behavior

Taking a telephone message is good **behavior**. It is a polite way to act.

Helen Keller

Read and Comprehend

Go Digital

☑ TARGET SKILL

Author's Purpose Authors write for many reasons. The reason an author writes something is called the **author's purpose.** You can look for text evidence as you read to help you figure out if the author wrote to make you smile, to tell you facts, or to explain ideas. You can list the text evidence on a chart like this one.

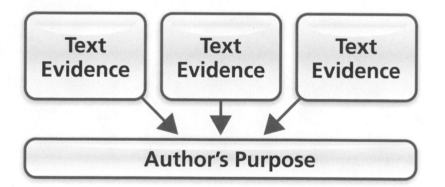

Text Evidence → Text Evidence → Text Evidence → Author's Purpose

☑ TARGET STRATEGY

Summarize As you read, stop to tell important ideas in your own words.

Special Ways to Communicate

People share their thoughts and ideas in different ways. Many people share ideas through talking or writing. Tools such as phones and computers can help people to communicate.

People who cannot hear or see have special ways to communicate. In *Helen Keller*, you will read about a girl who cannot see, hear, or talk. She must learn to communicate in other ways.

ANCHOR TEXT

Helen Keller

✓ TARGET SKILL

Author's Purpose Tell why an author writes a selection.

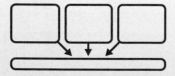

✓ GENRE

A **biography** tells about events in a person's life. As you read, look for:

▶ information about why a person is important

▶ events in time order

LACC.2.RI.1.3 describe the connection between a series of historical events/scientific ideas/steps in technical procedures; **LACC.2.RI.2.6** identify the main purpose of a text; **LACC.2.RI.4.10** read and comprehend informational texts

Go Digital

MEET THE AUTHOR

Jane Sutcliffe

The library was Jane Sutcliffe's favorite place to visit when she was a child. She says she loved reading biographies "just to get a peek at how other people lived day to day, in different times and places." Now she writes biographies.

MEET THE ILLUSTRATOR

Robert Papp

Most of Robert Papp's clothes are covered in oil paint. That's because he's extremely messy when he paints. Mr. Papp lives in Pennsylvania with his wife, Lisa, who is also an artist. She's not quite as messy as he is, though.

Helen Keller

by Jane Sutcliffe

selection illustrated by Robert Papp

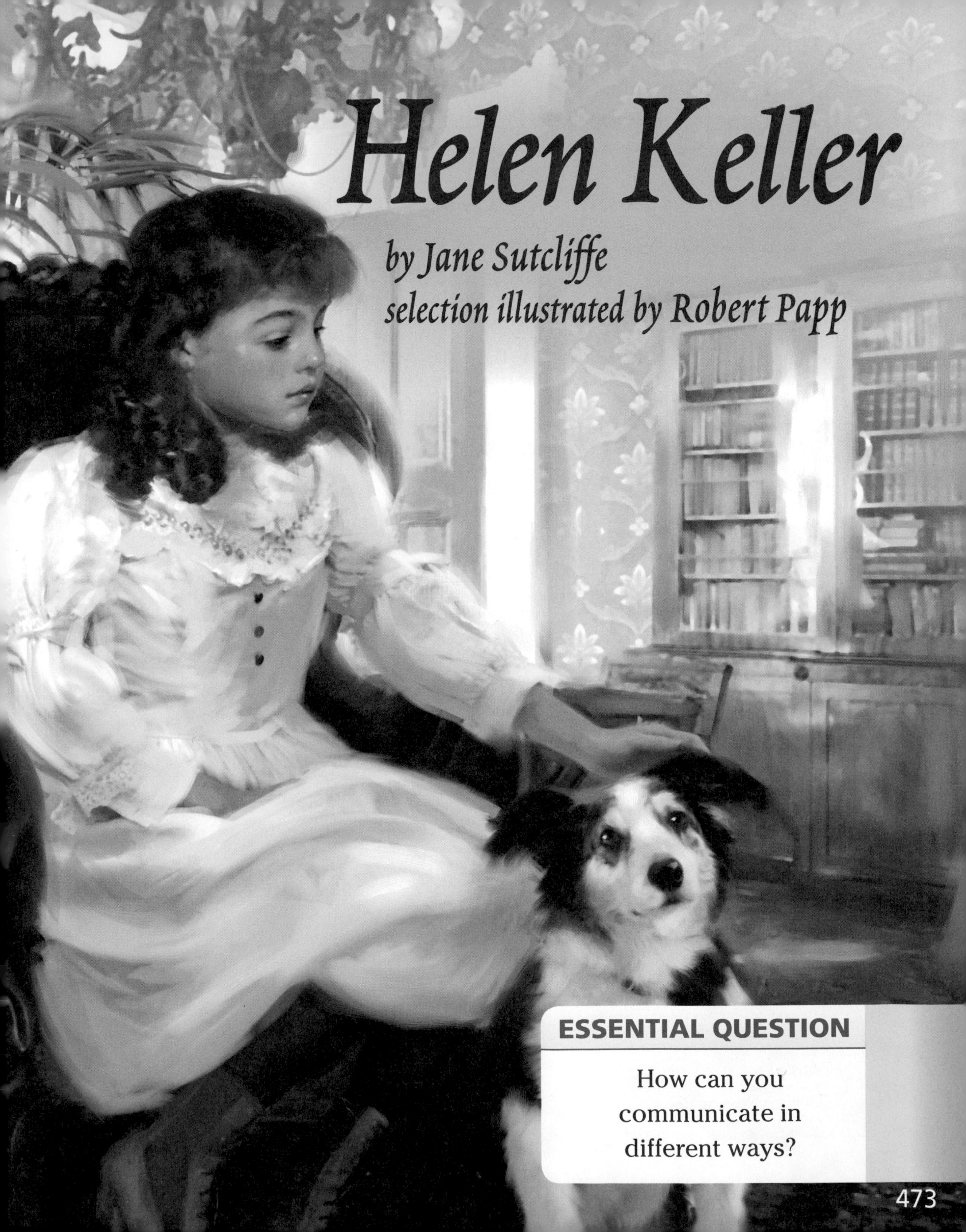

ESSENTIAL QUESTION

How can you communicate in different ways?

Tuscumbia, Alabama
1886

Helen Keller reached out. She touched warm, coarse hair. Her busy fingers moved farther down. They felt something smooth and wet. Slap! A hairy tail smacked into Helen's face.

Helen could not see her family's milking cow. But she liked touching it. Helen Keller had been blind and deaf for most of her life. The only way she knew the world was by touch, taste, and smell.

Helen was born in 1880 in Tuscumbia, Alabama. When she was just a baby, she became very sick. The illness took away her sight and hearing. Helen could not hear her brothers' laughter or her mother's voice. She could not see her father's smile or the pretty flowers outside her window. For Helen, there was only silence and gray darkness.

To learn to speak, children need to hear words. But Helen could not hear anything. So she could not speak. Instead, she made motions. When she wanted her mother, she put her hand against her face. When she wanted her father, she made the motion of putting on a pair of glasses. When she was hungry, she pretended to slice and butter bread.

Helen Keller

Helen knew she was different from the rest
of her family. They moved their lips when they
wanted things. Sometimes Helen stood between
two people as they talked. She held her hands to
their lips. Then she tried moving her own lips.
But still no one understood her.

That made Helen angry. Sometimes she
screamed and cried and kicked for hours.
She threw things and hit people. But it didn't
change anything. She was still alone in silence
and darkness.

Helen was hard to control. Her parents didn't know how to help her. They took her to doctors. None of the doctors could help Helen see or hear again. When Helen was six, a doctor suggested the Kellers visit Alexander Graham Bell. Dr. Bell was famous for inventing the telephone. He also taught deaf people.

Alexander Graham Bell

Dr. Bell told the Kellers to write to Michael Anagnos in Boston. Mr. Anagnos was the head of the Perkins Institution for the Blind. He believed Helen could learn how to let out the thoughts locked inside her. Mr. Anagnos promised to send Helen a teacher.

Michael Anagnos

Helen and Teacher
March 1887

Helen's teacher came to live with the Kellers that spring. Her name was Annie Sullivan. Annie had studied at the Perkins School. She was nearly blind herself. Annie needed to control Helen's wild behavior so she could teach her. But Helen did not understand that Annie wanted to help her. For two weeks, Helen fought with Annie. She hit Annie and knocked out one of her front teeth. She even locked Annie in an upstairs room. Mr. Keller had to get a ladder and let Annie out through a window.

Annie Sullivan

Still, Annie did not give up. Little by little, Helen learned to trust her new teacher. Annie began to teach Helen about words. She spelled words using her fingers. Her hand formed a different shape for each letter. She pressed each shape into Helen's hand. When she gave Helen some cake, she spelled C-A-K-E into Helen's palm. When Helen held her doll, Annie spelled D-O-L-L for Helen. Helen imitated the shapes. She thought it was a game. She didn't know that the shapes spelled words.

After a month, Helen could spell whatever Annie spelled. But Helen still did not know that she was naming the things she touched.

Annie finger spelling into Helen's hand

One day Helen and Annie walked to the well house. Someone was pumping water. Annie pushed Helen's hand into the rushing water. Helen felt the cool water on one hand. She felt her teacher's fingers spelling W-A-T-E-R into her other hand. Over and over, Annie spelled the word. Suddenly Helen stood very still. All at once she understood! The liquid flowing over her hand had a name. It was W-A-T-E-R!

ANALYZE THE TEXT

Genre: Biography How is learning that all things have a name an important event in Helen's life?

Everything had a name! Helen wanted to learn them all. She ran from one thing to another. Annie spelled the name of everything Helen touched. Then Helen turned and pointed to Annie. T-E-A-C-H-E-R, spelled Annie. From then on, Helen's name for Annie was "Teacher." That summer, Helen learned a lot of new words. She stopped using her old motions. Her fingers gave her all the words she needed.

Annie did not teach Helen words one at a time. She talked to her in full sentences. That way, Helen learned more than just new words. She learned new ideas. Helen and Annie took long walks through the woods and along the river. Annie gave Helen lessons on the walks. She showed Helen how seeds sprout and plants grow. She made mountains out of mud and taught Helen about volcanoes. Sometimes they climbed a tree and had a lesson there.

Helen and Annie having a lesson

Reading a book in Braille

Helen was hungry for knowledge. She wanted to learn everything Annie could teach her. Soon Annie started teaching Helen how to read. The words were printed in raised letters for a blind person.

Helen felt the words with her fingers. She liked to hunt for words she knew. When she learned to read better, she read her books over and over. Her curious fingers wore down the raised letters.

ANALYZE THE TEXT

Author's Purpose What is the author's purpose for writing about Helen Keller? Use text evidence to support your answer.

Helen also learned to write. She wrote letters to her family and Dr. Bell. She wrote many letters to Mr. Anagnos in Boston. Mr. Anagnos was amazed by how much Helen had learned. He published some of Helen's letters. Reporters began to write about Helen. Soon she was famous. People all over the world wanted to know about the miracle girl. And Helen wanted to know all about the world.

Dig Deeper

How to Analyze the Text

Use these pages to learn about Author's Purpose and Biographies. Then read *Helen Keller* again. Use what you learn to understand it better.

Author's Purpose

In *Helen Keller*, you read about real events that happened to a girl who was deaf and blind. The author had a reason for writing about Helen. An author's reason for writing is the **author's purpose.**

You can use details as text evidence to figure out why the author wrote *Helen Keller*. Use a chart like the one below to help you.

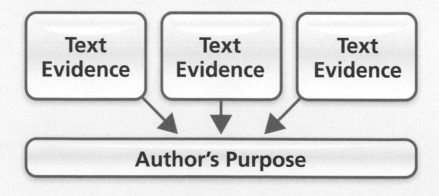

LACC.2.RI.1.3 describe the connection between a series of historical events/scientific ideas/steps in technical procedures; **LACC.2.RI.2.6** identify the main purpose of a text

Genre: Biography

Helen Keller is a **biography**. It tells about events in an important person's life. When you read a biography, think about how the events are connected. For example, Helen put her hands to people's lips as they spoke and then moved her lips. This helps you understand that Helen wanted to be able to communicate.

Your Turn

How can you communicate in different ways? Look for text evidence in *Helen Keller* to help you answer. Talk about your ideas with a partner. Listen carefully and take turns speaking. Add your own ideas to what your partner says.

💬 Classroom Conversation

Now talk about these questions with the class.

1. Why did Annie Sullivan keep working with Helen even though it was so difficult?

2. What makes Helen Keller an important person?

3. How are Annie Sullivan and Helen Keller alike? How are they different?

WRITE ABOUT READING

Response Who was a bigger hero, Helen or her teacher? Write a paragraph to tell your opinion. Use text evidence to explain your choice.

Writing Tip

Use end marks when you write. Remember that a statement ends with a period.

 COMMON CORE **LACC.2.RI.1.1** ask and answer questions to demonstrate understanding of key details; **LACC.2.RI.1.2** identify the main topic of a multiparagraph text and the focus of specific paragraphs; **LACC.2.W.1.1** write opinion pieces; **LACC.2.SL.1.1.a** follow rules for discussions; **LACC.2.SL.1.1.b** build on others' talk in conversations by linking comments to others' remarks

INFORMATIONAL TEXT

Informational text gives facts about a topic. This is a science text.

Photographs can be used to show ideas in a text. **Captions** tell more information about the photos.

LACC.2.RI.2.5 know and use text features to locate facts or information; **LACC.2.RI.3.7** explain how images contribute to and clarify text; **LACC.2.RI.4.10** read and comprehend informational texts

Helen Keller lived in darkness, but she was curious about the world. Braille helped Keller gain knowledge. Today people who cannot see still use Braille to help them read.

Many ATMs (Automated Teller Machines) have Braille labels, for example. That way, blind people can use them to do their banking.

Some ATMs even talk! With just one quick motion, users plug headphones into the ATM. Then the ATM tells them what to do.

A Braille notetaker is a computer that helps people who cannot see. They type their notes on it, using a Braille keyboard. The notes are saved in Braille. Later they can use their fingers to read the notes in silence on the notepad. The machine can also read the notes aloud!

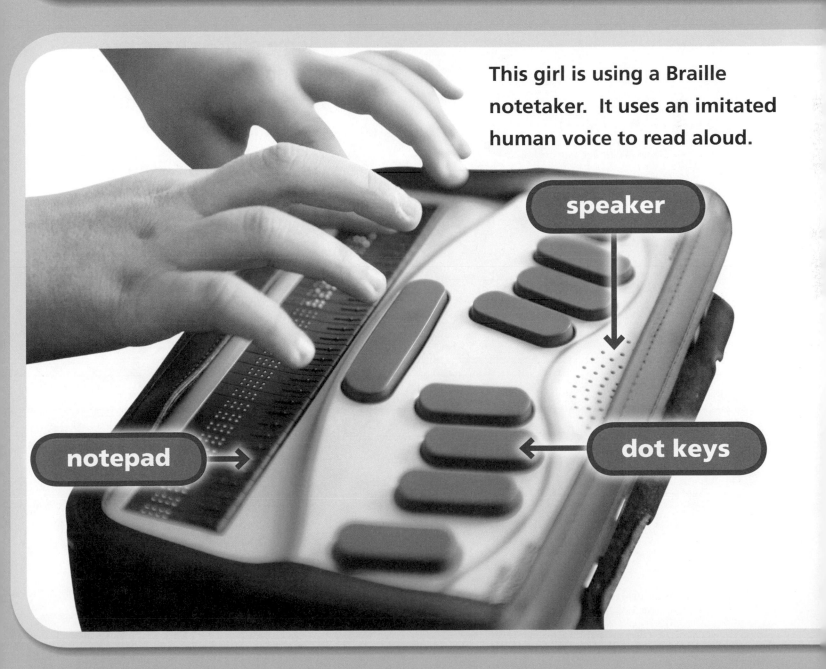

This girl is using a Braille notetaker. It uses an imitated human voice to read aloud.

speaker

notepad

dot keys

What if someone who cannot see has an illness and needs to take a temperature? Use a talking thermometer! There are talking clocks and watches as well. These watches often have Braille faces, too.

If Helen Keller were alive today, she'd be happy to learn of the many ways technology can help people with vision disabilities.

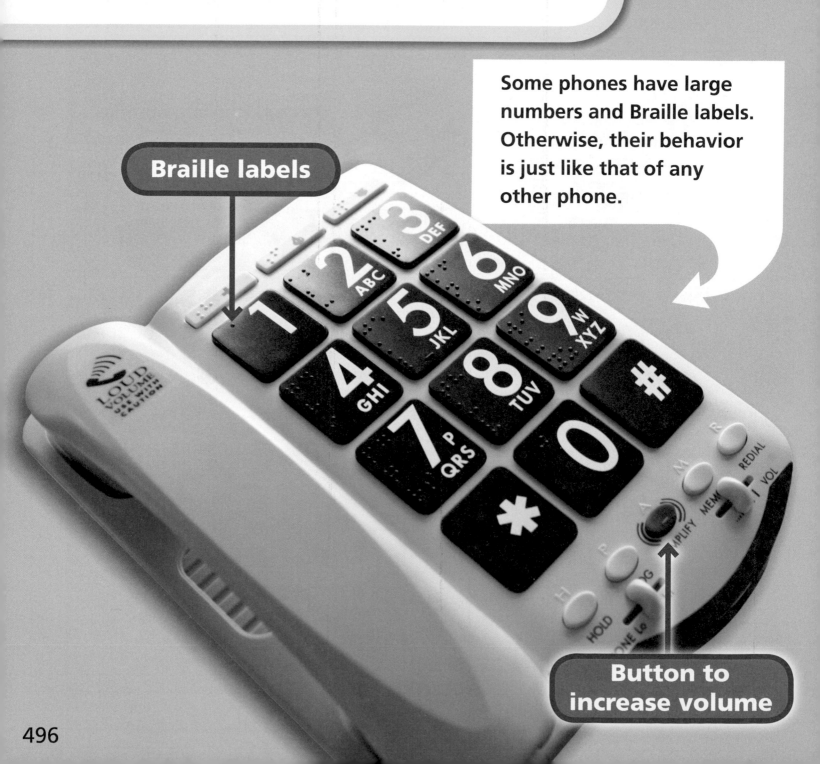

Some phones have large numbers and Braille labels. Otherwise, their behavior is just like that of any other phone.

Braille labels

Button to increase volume

Compare Texts

TEXT TO TEXT

Discuss Tools Could Helen Keller have used any of the tools from *Talking Tools?* Why or why not? Discuss your ideas with a partner.

TEXT TO SELF

Share Experiences Think of some things that Annie Sullivan taught Helen Keller. Talk with a group about the way you learned these same lessons and how that is different from the way Helen learned them. Take turns listening and speaking. Ask a question if you do not understand your classmates' ideas.

TEXT TO WORLD

Making Changes Compare the Braille book on page 487 with the Braille tools in *Talking Tools*. What changes have we made to machines so that people who cannot see can also use them?

COMMON CORE **LACC.2.RI.1.1** ask and answer questions to demonstrate understanding of key details; **LACC.2.RI.3.7** explain how images contribute to and clarify text; **LACC.2.RI.3.9** compare and contrast points presented by two texts on same topic; **LACC.2.SL.1.1.a** follow rules for discussions

Grammar

Using Proper Nouns Names for **days** of the week and **months** of the year begin with capital letters. Each important word in the name of a **holiday** begins with a capital letter, too.

Days	Months	Holidays
Monday	March	New Year's Day
Friday	July	Thanksgiving Day
Saturday	September	Fourth of July

Try This! **Write each sentence correctly.**

❶ Is labor day in september?

❷ valentine's day is in february.

❸ This monday is earth day.

❹ I gave my mother flowers on mother's day.

In your writing, use days, holidays, and dates to tell your reader more about when things happen. Remember to begin the names of days, months, and holidays with a capital letter.

Without Words That Tell When	With Words That Tell When
I read books to a neighbor. She lost her sight.	Every Sunday I read books to a neighbor. She lost her sight on May 25, 2007.

 ## Connect Grammar to Writing

As you revise your persuasive essay next week, think about ways to tell your reader more. Add words that tell when.

Reading-Writing Workshop: Prewrite

Opinion Writing

✓ **Ideas** When you write to persuade, give your readers reasons to support your opinion and goal.

Farah made a web to plan her **persuasive essay**. She had two reasons. Later, she added details and facts to make her reasons stronger.

Writing Process Checklist

▶ **Prewrite**

☑ **Did I choose a goal I care about?**

☑ **Did I give reasons that support my opinion and goal?**

☑ **Did I include details and facts to make my reasons convincing to my audience?**

Draft

Revise

Edit

Publish and Share

Exploring a Topic

Goal:
Raise Money for
Braille Books

Library needs more Braille books

We can help

```
               Goal: Raise Money
                for Braille Books

      Library needs more              We can help
         Braille books

   Many        Library      Our school      We can
   people      has only      wants a        do a
   in town    20 Braille    community     read-a-thon
    read        books        project
   Braille
```

Reading as a Writer

What details did Farah add? What details can you add to make your reasons more persuasive?

I added supporting details to make my reasons more convincing.

OFFICER BUCKLE AND GLORIA

PEGGY RATHMANN

Safety at Home

✓ TARGET VOCABULARY

obeys

safety

attention

buddy

station

speech

shocked

enormous

Vocabulary Reader

Training a Dog

Context Cards

COMMON CORE
LACC.2.L.3.6 use words and phrases acquired through conversations, reading and being read to, and responding to texts

Go Digital

Vocabulary in Context

▶ Read each Context Card.

▶ Tell a story about two pictures using the Vocabulary words.

1 **obeys**

A careful driver always obeys traffic rules. This driver stops at a stop sign.

2 **safety**

The firefighter talks about fire safety. He teaches about staying out of danger.

3 attention

Before crossing the street, stand at attention and look both ways.

4 buddy

Never swim alone. Always swim with a buddy, or friend.

5 station

A police station is a safe place to go if you need help.

6 speech

His job is to give a short speech. He will talk about airplane safety.

7 shocked

She is shocked at how hot it is outside. She needs to get out of the sun soon!

8 enormous

Only the workers can go inside the fence on this enormous work site.

Read and Comprehend

☑ **TARGET SKILL**

Cause and Effect In *Officer Buckle and Gloria*, one event makes another event happen. The first event is the **cause**. The event that happens because of the cause is the **effect**.

As you read a story, ask yourself what happens and why. Find answers by looking at the words and pictures in the story. You can use a chart like this to show how the events connect.

Cause	Effect

☑ **TARGET STRATEGY**

Monitor/Clarify If you don't understand why something is happening, stop and think. Find text evidence to figure out what doesn't make sense.

COMMON CORE **LACC.2.RL.1.1** ask and answer questions to demonstrate understanding of key details; **LACC.2.RL.1.3** describe how characters respond to events and challenges; **LACC.2.RL.3.7** use information from illustrations and words to demonstrate understanding of characters, setting, or plot

Personal Safety

It is important to stay safe. You should wear a helmet when you ride your bike. You also should look both ways before crossing a street. These are just two things to do to be safe. Parents, teachers, and police officers can help you learn more about safety.

Officer Buckle is a police officer who loves sharing safety tips. You will read about Officer Buckle and his helpful dog in *Officer Buckle and Gloria*.

ANCHOR TEXT

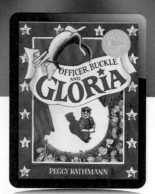

✓ TARGET SKILL

Cause and Effect Tell how one event makes another happen.

✓ GENRE

Humorous fiction is a story that is written to make the reader laugh. As you read, look for:

▶ characters who do or say funny things

▶ events that would not happen in real life

COMMON CORE LACC.2.RL.1.1 ask and answer questions to demonstrate understanding of key details; LACC.2.RL.3.7 use information from illustrations and words to demonstrate understanding of characters, setting, or plot; LACC.2.RL.4.10 read and comprehend literature

MEET THE AUTHOR AND ILLUSTRATOR

PEGGY RATHMANN

Peggy Rathmann's family had a dog named Skippy. One holiday they were gathered for breakfast. A family member was filming them. It wasn't until later when they were watching the home movie that they caught Skippy in the background, licking the poached eggs on the serving table. No one had seen it happen. Skippy was the model for the dog in *Officer Buckle and Gloria.*

OFFICER BUCKLE
AND
GLORIA

written and illustrated by
PEGGY RATHMANN

ESSENTIAL QUESTION

Why is it important to follow safety rules?

Officer Buckle knew more safety tips than anyone else in Napville.

Every time he thought of a new one, he thumbtacked it to his bulletin board.

Safety Tip #77
NEVER stand on a SWIVEL CHAIR.

Officer Buckle shared his safety tips with the students at Napville School.

Nobody ever listened.

Sometimes, there was snoring.

Afterward, it was business as usual.

Mrs. Toppel, the principal, took down the welcome banner.

"NEVER stand on a SWIVEL CHAIR," said Officer Buckle, but Mrs. Toppel didn't hear him.

Then one day, Napville's police department bought a police dog named Gloria.

When it was time for Officer Buckle to give the safety speech at the school, Gloria went along.

"Children, this is Gloria," announced Officer Buckle. "Gloria obeys my commands. Gloria, SIT!" And Gloria sat.

Officer Buckle gave Safety Tip Number One:
"KEEP your SHOELACES tied!"
The children sat up and stared.

Officer Buckle checked to see if Gloria was
sitting at attention. She was.

"Safety Tip Number Two," said Officer Buckle.
"ALWAYS wipe up spills BEFORE someone SLIPS
AND FALLS!"

The children's eyes popped.

Officer Buckle checked on Gloria again.

"Good dog," he said.

Officer Buckle thought of a safety tip he had
discovered that morning.

"NEVER leave a THUMBTACK where you might SIT on it!"

The audience roared.

Officer Buckle grinned. He said the rest of
the tips with *plenty* of expression.

The children clapped their hands and
cheered. Some of them laughed until they cried.

Officer Buckle was surprised. He had never
noticed how funny safety tips could be.

After *this* safety speech, there wasn't a
single accident.

ANALYZE THE TEXT

Cause and Effect What do
the children do when Gloria
acts out Officer Buckle's
safety tips?

The next day, an enormous envelope arrived
at the police station. It was stuffed with thank-you
letters from the students at Napville School.

Every letter had a drawing of Gloria on it.

Officer Buckle thought the drawings showed a
lot of imagination.

His favorite letter was written on a star-shaped piece of paper. It said:

You and Gloria make a good team.

Your friend,
Claire

P.S. I always wear a crash helmet.
(Safety Tip #7)

Officer Buckle was thumbtacking Claire's letter to his bulletin board when the phones started ringing. Grade schools, high schools, and day-care centers were calling about the safety speech.

"Officer Buckle," they said, "our students want to hear your safety tips! And please, bring along that police dog."

Officer Buckle told his safety tips to 313 schools.
Everywhere he and Gloria went, children sat up
and listened.

After every speech, Officer Buckle took Gloria out for ice cream.

Officer Buckle loved having a buddy.

Then one day, a television news team videotaped Officer Buckle in the state-college auditorium.

When he finished Safety Tip Number Ninety-nine, DO NOT GO SWIMMING DURING ELECTRICAL STORMS!, the students jumped to their feet and applauded.

"Bravo! Bravo!" they cheered. Officer
Buckle bowed again and again.

That night, Officer Buckle watched himself
on the 10 o'clock news.

The next day, the principal of Napville School
telephoned the police station.

"Good morning, Officer Buckle! It's time for
our safety speech!"

Officer Buckle frowned.

"I'm not giving any more speeches! Nobody
looks at me, anyway!"

"Oh," said Mrs. Toppel. "Well! How about
Gloria? Could she come?"

Someone else from the police station gave Gloria a ride to the school.

Gloria sat onstage looking lonely. Then she fell asleep. So did the audience.

After Gloria left, Napville School had its biggest accident ever . . .

It started with a puddle of banana pudding. . . .
SPLAT! SPLATTER! SPLOOSH!

Everyone slid smack into Mrs. Toppel, who screamed and let go of her hammer.

ANALYZE THE TEXT

Humor What happens when the people don't follow Officer Buckle's tips? How does the author make what happens seem funny?

The next morning, a pile of letters arrived at the police station.

Every letter had a drawing of the accident.

Officer Buckle was shocked.

At the bottom of the pile was a note written on a paper star.

Officer Buckle smiled. The note said:

Gloria gave Officer Buckle a big kiss on the nose.

Officer Buckle gave Gloria a nice pat on the back.

Then, Officer Buckle thought of his best safety tip yet . . .

Safety Tip #101

"ALWAYS STICK WITH YOUR BUDDY!"

Dig Deeper

How to Analyze the Text

Use these pages to learn about Cause and Effect and Humor. Then read *Officer Buckle and Gloria* again. Use what you learn to understand it better.

Cause and Effect

Officer Buckle and Gloria is a funny story about a police officer and his dog, Gloria. In this story, one event makes another happen. For example, Gloria does tricks behind Officer Buckle. As a result, the audience laughs. Gloria's tricks are the **cause**. The audience's laughter is the **effect**.

As you read, think about what happens and why. Use a chart like the one below to show causes and effects.

Cause	Effect

LACC.2.RL.1.1 ask and answer questions to demonstrate understanding of key details; **LACC.2.RL.1.3** describe how characters respond to events and challenges; **LACC.2.RL.3.7** use information from illustrations and words to demonstrate understanding of characters, setting, or plot

Humor

The author of a **humorous fiction** story wants to make the reader laugh. The author may have a character do or say something that is funny. The pictures may also show something funny.

In *Officer Buckle and Gloria*, the safety tips that Officer Buckle gives are serious. Gloria acts out the tips in a funny way. As you read, ask yourself questions about the words and pictures to figure out if the author is trying to be funny or not.

Your Turn

 Why is it important to follow safety rules? Look for ideas in the words and pictures in *Officer Buckle and Gloria*. Share your ideas with a small group. Take turns adding your own ideas to what others say.

Classroom Conversation

Now talk about these questions with the class.

1 What events in the story cause other events to happen?

2 How is Gloria different from real police dogs?

3 How might the children at the schools change after Officer Buckle and Gloria visit? Tell why you think so.

WRITE ABOUT READING

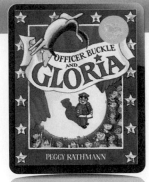

Response Do you think that the story is funny? Why or why not? Write a paragraph to explain your opinion. Use story words and pictures as evidence to help explain your ideas.

Writing Tip

Remember to start the name of each person and each proper noun with a capital letter.

LACC.2.RL.1.3 describe how characters respond to events and challenges; **LACC.2.RL.3.7** use information from illustrations and words to demonstrate understanding of characters, setting, or plot; **LACC.2.W.1.1** write opinion pieces; **LACC.2.SL.1.1.a** follow rules for discussions; **LACC.2.SL.1.1.b** build on others' talk in conversations by linking comments to others' remarks

Readers'
Theater

☑ GENRE

Readers' Theater is a text that has been written for readers to read aloud.

☑ TEXT FOCUS

Dialogue is the talk between characters in a play. Dialogue helps readers get to know the characters through their own words.

Safety at Home

by Margaret Sweeny

**Cast of
Characters**

Dad

Alexa

Jake

LACC.2.RL.2.6 acknowledge differences in points of view of characters; **LACC.2.RL.4.10** read and comprehend literature

Dad: What did you do on your class trip?

Alexa: We visited an enormous fire station.

Jake: The fire chief gave a speech about fire safety.

Dad: I hope you were paying attention.

Alexa: We were. Later, we worked with a buddy to make a safety poster. I worked with Jake.

Jake: Look at our poster.

STOP, DROP, AND ROLL

1. If your clothes catch on fire, don't run.
2. **STOP** where you are.
3. **DROP** to the ground. Cover your face with your hands.
4. **ROLL** over and over to put out the fire.

Dad: I'm shocked! You know more about fire safety than I do.

Alexa: Everyone in our school obeys fire safety rules.

Jake: Guess what **get low and go** means?

Alexa: If the house is smoky, get low.

Jake: That's because smoke rises. Get low to stay below the smoke.

Alexa: Crawl to the nearest way out.

Jake: Then go to a safe meeting place to wait for your family.

Dad: Let's pick a meeting place right now!

Compare Texts

TEXT TO TEXT

Compare and Contrast How is the message in *Officer Buckle and Gloria* like the message in *Safety at Home?* How are they different?

TEXT TO SELF

Write a Caption Officer Buckle's safety tips are based on his own life. Think of a safety tip you know. Draw a picture of what Gloria might do to act out that tip. Then write a caption for your picture.

TEXT TO WORLD

Connect to Social Studies Gloria acted out safety tips, and Alexa and Jake made a fire safety poster. Make a poster of classroom safety tips or act them out for your class.

 LACC.2.RL.1.2 recount stories and determine their message, lesson, or moral

Grammar

Abbreviations The names of days, months, and places are proper nouns that can be shortened. An **abbreviation** is a short way to write a word by taking out some of the letters and writing a period at the end. Abbreviations for proper nouns begin with a capital letter.

Proper Nouns	Abbreviations
Monday	Mon.
March	Mar.
Main Street	Main St.

 **Write the proper noun for each abbreviation.**

❶ Nov.　　❹ Canton St.

❷ Tues.　　❺ Jan.

❸ Elm Rd.　　❻ Fri.

Write abbreviations correctly. Remember
to use a period at the end of an abbreviation.
Capitalize the abbreviation for a proper noun.

Incorrect	Correct
mr Wang says the police officer will visit our class on sept 4.	Mr. Wang says the police officer will visit our class on Sept. 4.

 ## Connect Grammar to Writing

When you edit your persuasive essay, make sure you have used capital letters and end marks correctly.

LACC.2.W.1.1 write opinion pieces

Reading-Writing Workshop: Revise

Opinion Writing

☑ **Organization** When you write a **persuasive essay**, each reason can start a new paragraph.

Farah wrote a draft of her essay. Later, she moved things around so each reason started a new paragraph. She also added more linking words, such as *so, also,* and *because,* to link her opinions to her reasons.

Writing Process Checklist

Prewrite

Draft

▶ **Revise**

  ☑ Did I tell my goal in a clear way?

  ☑ Did I give reasons for my goal?

  ☑ Did I include facts and examples for each reason?

  ☑ Did I sum up my reasons?

Edit

Publish and Share

Revised Draft

Our town library has a problem that we must fix. ¶ The town library does not have enough Braille books for people who need them. It needs money for Braille books.

There are thirty-four people in our town who read Braille. The library has only twenty Braille books, so it needs more books.

Help Our Library!

by Farah Jamali

Our town library has a problem that we must fix. It needs money for Braille books.

The town library does not have enough Braille books for the people who need them. There are thirty-four people in our town who read Braille. The library has only twenty Braille books, so it needs more.

Our school should help the library by having a read-a-thon. Each student can fill out a pledge sheet. The money we raise could buy the Braille books our community needs.

Reading as a Writer

How did Farah organize her essay to make her reasons clearer? How can you organize your reasons and details?

I started a new paragraph for each reason.

**Read "Austin's Famous Flyers" and "Bats."
As you read, stop and answer each question.**

Austin's Famous Flyers

Every summer night, hundreds of people gather around a bridge in Austin, Texas. They are there to see the bats!

> **1** How does the photograph help you better understand what you just read?

Builders fixed the bridge in 1980. Soon after, bats began moving in by the thousands. At first, many people in Austin were not happy. Many were afraid of the bats.

Then they learned the surprising news. Healthy bats are not dangerous. They are harmless and even helpful. The group of bats that lives under this bridge can eat up to 20,000 pounds of insects each night. This includes insects that bite people and insects that eat crops. Now the bridge is the home to more than a million bats in the summer. People come from all over to see Austin's famous bats.

> **2** How did the people in the article change? What reasons does the author give for this change?

COMMON CORE

LACC.2.RI.2.5 know and use text features to locate facts or information; LACC.2.RI.3.7 explain how images contribute to and clarify text; LACC.2.RI.3.8 describe how reasons support points the author makes; LACC.2.RI.3.9 compare and contrast points presented by two texts on same topic; LACC.2.RI.4.10 read and comprehend informational texts

Bats

About Bats

Bats are mammals. They live on every continent in the world except Antarctica. Most bats live where it is warm. There are almost 50 kinds of bats in the United States.

Helpful Bats

Some people don't like bats. They are afraid of them. Bats are not harmful to people. In fact, bats are helpful!

Most bats help us by eating small flying bugs. Some of the bugs are harmful to people. Some bats can eat as many as 2,000 bugs in a night! We would see a lot more bugs if bats weren't around to eat them.

Other kinds of bats eat fruit. These bats eat the fruit and drop the seeds. This helps to put seeds in new places so more fruit will grow. This helps other animals have food, too.

Some bats help farmers. They eat worms that live in corn fields. If the bats didn't eat these pests, the corn would die. That would mean less corn for us!

> **3** Which heading on this page would you look under if you wanted to read about how bats help people?

Helping the Bats

Some people build bat houses in their yard. The bats come to stay in them. This gives the bats a safe place to live. It also helps the person get rid of bugs!

❹ What information in this article is the same as in "Austin's Famous Flyers"? What is different or new?

Glossary

This glossary can help you find the meanings of some of the words in this book. The meanings given are the meanings of the words as they are used in the book. Sometimes a second meaning is also given.

A

attend

To look carefully at or take care of: *We try to **attend** to the work we are asked to do.*

attention

A form of **attend:** *They stood at **attention** to show they were listening.*

B

beak

A bill, or the hard mouth parts of a bird: *The baby birds opened their **beaks** wide, waiting for their food.*

behave

To act in a certain way: *We always tried to **behave** well when visitors were in the room.*

behavior

A form of **behave:** *His **behavior** in school was better than it was at home.*

believe

To accept as true or real: *I **believe** that you have the hat.*

bend

To become curved or not straight: *The tree branches **bend** down in the heavy snow.*

beak

beware

To be careful or look out for a problem: *The sign told us to* **beware** *of falling rocks.*

bloom

To blossom or grow into flower: *Some plants* **bloom** *in the spring, while others are just starting to grow.*

bloom

blooming

A form of **bloom:** *Butterflies come to the garden when that bush is* **blooming.**

brag

To boast, or speak with too much pride: *She tries not to* **brag** *about winning, but she wants us to know.*

branch

A part that grows out from a trunk of a tree: *All the* **branches** *of the tree had yellow leaves.*

break

To separate into pieces or tear apart: *We had to* **break** *the ground up with different garden tools.*

breeze

A light wind: *The puppy smelled smoke when she sniffed the* **breeze.**

buddy

A pal or close friend: *He became my* **buddy** *during our first summer in camp.*

burst

To be full to the point of breaking open: *She tried hard not to* **burst** *out laughing when she saw the silly hat.*

bursting

A form of **burst:** *The milkweed pod was bursting with silky seeds.*

bursting

C

canned

Something that was put in a can to help it stay fresh: *We eat canned fruit when we do not have any fresh fruit.*

chew

To grind or crush with teeth: *Chew your food carefully before you swallow.*

chews

A form of **chew:** *He chews gum a lot.*

choice

The act of choosing or the chance to choose: *We had many choices about what to see in the city.*

clipped

To be attached with a clip: *The two pieces of paper were clipped together so they would not get lost.*

coat

The fur or hair of an animal: *The dog's coat was wet after he went outside in the rain.*

collar

A leather, cloth, or metal band for an animal's neck: *Both of our dogs wear red collars around their necks.*

community

A group of people who live together in the same area: *Our **community** is filled with friendly neighbors.*

concentrate

To put all of your attention on one thing: *It was hard to **concentrate** on my homework because my brother was talking to me.*

cousin

A child of one's aunt or uncle: *My **cousin** stayed with us for two days.*

creative

To be good at making new things or having new ideas: *My teacher said that my art project was very different and **creative**.*

crown

A head covering that a queen, king, or other ruler might wear: *She used paper, glue, and glitter to make a **crown** for her costume.*

crown

culture

The traditions, arts, and beliefs of a certain group of people: *In his Native American **culture**, the fall harvest is a time for celebration.*

curious

Eager to find out or learn about something: *He was **curious** about many kinds of sea animals, so he loved the aquarium.*

curl

To make a rounded shape: *He showed us how to **curl** slices of carrot in cold water.*

curled

A form of **curl:** *The kitten **curled** up in his lap and purred happily.*

curly

A form of **curl:** *My brother's hair is so thick and **curly** he can hardly comb it.*

D

damage

To harm or injure: *The flood might **damage** the bridge so that it must be closed for repair.*

danger

The chance of harm, or something that may cause harm: *We had good reasons to worry about **danger** deep in the dark cave.*

dangerous

A form of **danger:** *The little rabbit knew it was a **dangerous** place, but she hopped closer.*

dark

Without light or with very little light: *With no moon, the night was **dark.***

darkness

A form of **dark:** *In the **darkness**, he couldn't tell what kind of animal was outside.*

decide

To make up one's mind: *Tomorrow I will **decide** what to do about the party.*

deep

Located far below the surface or far from an opening: *They buried the treasure **deep** in the ground near a pine tree.*

deepest

A form of **deep:** *In the **deepest** part of the ocean, it is very dark.*

demand

To ask firmly or to require: *The teachers in that school* **demand** *hard work from their students.*

direction

The place or line along which someone or something goes: *Walk in the* **direction** *of the town.*

direction

disgust

To cause a sick or bad feeling: *If those movies* **disgust** *you, please stop watching them.*

disgusting

A form of **disgust:** *When she sniffed at the garbage pail, it smelled* **disgusting**.

drift

To float along or be carried along on water or air: *Our raft will* **drift** *if we do not paddle.*

drool

To let saliva drip from the mouth: *My baby sister* **drools** *on my arm and makes my sleeve wet.*

drooled

A form of **drool:** *He* **drooled** *when he looked at all the delicious food.*

E

enormous

Huge, or very large in size: *Hank was an **enormous** dog, almost the size of a cow.*

enormous

equal

To be the same as: *Seven days **equal** one week, and twenty-four hours equal one day.*

expression

A certain mood or feeling that something has: *My sister's voice had a lot of **expression** as she read the funny poem.*

F

flash

To give out a sudden bright light: *The fireworks **flash** in the night sky, and people cheer.*

flash

flop

To drop or hang heavily: *When I'm really tired, I **flop** onto the couch for a nap.*

floppy

A form of **flop:** *Some rabbits have **floppy** ears that droop around their face.*

furious

Full of great anger, or raging: *She was so **furious** that she threw a pillow across the room.*

G

gather

To bring or come together in one place: *We will **gather** for the meeting at noon today.*

gathered

A form of **gather:** *After the whole group **gathered** on stage, they began to sing.*

H

hairy

Having a lot of hair: *It takes a long time to brush my dog because she is so **hairy**.*

hang

To be attached at the upper end: *Many colorful paintings **hang** on the walls of the museum.*

heal

To get better or become well: *Most cuts **heal** quickly if you take care of them.*

healed

A form of **heal:** *When the deer's leg **healed**, she ran as fast as ever.*

height

The distance from bottom to top: *The **height** of the mountain is about a mile above sea level.*

height

I

ill

Sick or not healthy: *They have been **ill** with the flu.*

illness

A form of **ill:** *After an **illness**, people may feel tired for a few days.*

imitate

To copy the actions, looks, or sounds of: *Little children **imitate** their parents or older children in their family.*

imitated

A form of **imitate:** *After I **imitated** the steps many times, I learned to do the dance.*

impatient

Not able or willing to wait: *She walked because she was too **impatient** to wait for the bus.*

impossible

Not possible or not able to happen: *It will be **impossible** to finish on time unless you start now.*

inform

To tell about something: *The guide **informs** people about animals on the nature trail.*

insect

A bug that has six legs, a body with three main parts, and, usually, wings: *She liked to watch **insects** at the pond.*

insect

J

judge

To listen or look at in order to decide about: *At the fair, it was fun to **judge** which pie should win the first prize.*

K

know

To understand or have the facts about: *Do you **know** what causes thunder?*

knowledge

Facts and ideas, or information: *Their teacher had **knowledge** about many subjects, such as weather and history.*

L

language

A system of words, expressions, signs, or symbols shared by a group of people: *At our house we speak two **languages**: Spanish and English.*

lesson

Something to be learned or taught: *After a few more **lessons**, I'll be able to skate like an Olympic athlete!*

litter

More than one animal born at the same time to the same mother: *My cat had a **litter** of four kittens.*

M

mammal

A warm-blooded animal with a backbone and hair: *Many animals, such as dogs and cats, are **mammals**.*

millions

A very large number, or more than a thousand thousands: *There are **millions** of fish in the sea.*

motion

Movement, gesture, or the act of moving: *The **motion** of the boat on the waves made him feel sleepy.*

muscle

Body tissue that helps many different parts of the body move and work: *Her **muscles** will get stronger from exercise.*

N

nod

To move the head down and up in a quick motion that may mean "okay": *You will be out of the game if you move before I **nod** my head.*

nodded

A form of **nod:** *I was glad when my father **nodded** to let us know we could go.*

noise

A sound that may be loud or unpleasant: *You could tell from the **noises** that there were many animals in the barn.*

noise

notice

To pay attention to or make note of: *I sat in the back and hoped that nobody would **notice** me.*

noticed

A form of **notice:** *The first thing he **noticed** was how fast the clouds moved across the sky.*

O

obey

To do what is asked: *After training, the horse **obeys** the rider.*

P

performance

A song, dance, or act that is given in front of an audience: *The singers were nervous before their first **performance** for the judges.*

piano
A musical instrument with a keyboard: *She could play tunes on the **piano**.*

piano

plain
Not fancy or pretty: *The plants look **plain** before they bloom.*

pond
A small body of water in the shape of a lake or pool: *Frogs sat at the edge of the **pond**.*

porch
A structure with a roof that is attached to the outside of a house: *They kept two chairs and a low table on the **porch**.*

pound
To hammer or hit hard again and again: *When you **pound** on the drum, I want to leave the room.*

pounding
A form of **pound**: *The **pounding** rain on the tent kept her from falling asleep.*

prevent
To stop or keep from happening: *You can **prevent** fires by being careful.*

problem
Something that is difficult to deal with or understand: *The group tried to solve the **problem** by talking together.*

Q

quiet
Silent, calm, or with hardly any sound: *The house was finally **quiet** after all the children were asleep.*

R

reach

To get to or go as far as: *When all the boats **reach** the shore, I will feel better.*

relieved

To no longer be worried about something or someone: *She was **relieved** that she did not miss the bus even though she was late.*

remember

To think of again or bring back in the mind: *I **remember** the first word I learned to read.*

remembered

A form of **remember**: *He always **remembered** his grandpa's stories.*

rotten

Decayed or spoiled: *Some insects eat **rotten** fruit that people throw away.*

row

In a line or in sequence, one after another: *I got an A on two tests in a **row**, which is a new record for me!*

S

safe

Free from danger or harm: *The mother bird saw that her babies were **safe** in the nest.*

safe

safety

A form of **safe**: *Most playground rules were made for your **safety**.*

scare

To frighten or make afraid: *This dragon mask might **scare** some little children.*

scent

A special smell that comes from something: *The **scent** of roses reminded her of her grandmother's yard in the spring.*

scent

scream

To make a long, loud, high-pitched cry: *When my little sister **screams**, I hold my ears.*

screaming

A form of **scream:** *When the game got close, many people started **screaming** for their team to win.*

shape

To give a certain form or shape to: *I **shape** the clay to look like woodland animals.*

shaped

A form of **shape:** *The sign at the farm stand was large and **shaped** like a pumpkin.*

share

To divide with others or take part in: *He wanted to **share** his story with us.*

shock

To surprise or greatly upset: *The news will **shock** you, so please sit down.*

shocked

A form of **shock:** *I was **shocked** when I found that the jewels were missing.*

shovel

A tool with a long handle and a flattened scoop: *We use **shovels** to get rid of the snow.*

shovel

silence

A form of **silent:** *The **silence** in the library helps people enjoy their reading.*

silent

Quiet, making or having no sound: *The room was **silent**, so she thought everyone had gone.*

simple

Easy, or not complicated: *The directions on the box looked **simple**, and she followed them carefully.*

special

Different from what is common or usual: *Birthdays are **special** occasions.*

speech

The act of speaking, or a talk: *She practiced at home before she gave the **speech** in class.*

spend

To cause or allow time to pass: *We will **spend** the day at the beach.*

sprinkle

To scatter in drops or small pieces: *We always **sprinkle** salt into the water before it boils.*

sprinkled

A form of **sprinkle:** *The children **sprinkled** fish food into the goldfish bowl.*

stand

To be a certain height: *Medium-size dogs usually stand between two and three feet tall.*

station

A place where a special service is provided: *We got our tickets and waited at the train station.*

station

stay

To live with or visit for an amount of time: *Please stay at my house after school.*

stayed

A form of **stay**: *We stayed at my friend's party for two hours.*

stick

To attach or to keep in one place: *We stick a stamp on each card before we mail it.*

sticky

Holding together as with glue or hard to pull apart: *After eating the honey, they licked their sticky fingers.*

stood

A form of **stand**: *Last year my sister stood three feet tall, but now she's almost four feet.*

straight

Not curving, curling, or bending: *My hair is straight and never gets wavy.*

stuck

A form of **stick**: *The truck got stuck in the heavy snow.*

subject

Course of study: *Science and social studies are his favorite subjects in school.*

sudden

Happening or coming without warning: *On the hike, we were caught in a **sudden** storm.*

suddenly

A form of **sudden:** *The birds flew away as **suddenly** as they had landed in the yard.*

T

tease

To make fun of or try to bother: *My friends used to **tease** me about my hair.*

tough

Strong and not likely to break or wear out: *The hiking boots were warm and **tough**, so he could walk outdoors in any weather.*

toward

In the direction of: *We walked **toward** the tower and watched for a light.*

transportation

Means of getting from one place to another: *Trains are my favorite kind of **transportation**.*

tune

A group of musical notes that are put together: *We had fun making up a new **tune** to play on the piano.*

tunnel

A passage underground or underwater: *The train passed through the **tunnel** to the other side of the mountain.*

tunnel

U

understand

To get the meaning of:
*I **understand** the meaning of a few Spanish words.*

V

vibration

A quick movement back and forth: *I could see the **vibration** of the cymbals as the musician hit them together.*

visit

To go or come to see: *We will **visit** our friends in the city.*

volume

An amount of sound: *You should speak in a quite **volume** when in the library.*

W

weak

Having little or no power, strength, or energy: *The battery was so **weak** that our flashlight didn't help much.*

weaker

A form of **weak**: *She was **weaker** after being sick, but then she grew stronger.*

wear

To have on the body: *In cold places, people **wear** two or three layers of clothes.*

weigh

Find out the weight or heaviness of: *The doctor will **weigh** you on a scale before your checkup.*

weighed

A form of **weigh**: *I **weighed** my dog three times to make sure she was really that heavy!*

wind

To move along with twists and turns: *We **wind** the string around the stick to bring the kite back in.*

winding

A form of **wind:** *They followed a **winding** path higher and higher up the mountain.*

winding

wonder

A marvel or something amazing: *Their tricks on the high wire were a **wonder** to everyone who watched.*

wonderful

A form of **wonder:** *Their day at the beach was **wonderful** from beginning to end.*

wrap

To cover by winding or folding: ***Wrap** a scarf around your neck before you go out in the cold wind.*

wrapped

A form of **wrap:** *We **wrapped** our sandwiches in foil for the picnic.*

wrapped

wrinkle

To form small, uneven lines or creases: *This cloth will **wrinkle** after you wash it, so you will need an iron.*

wrinkled

A form of **wrinkle:** *The shirt was **wrinkled**, so she tried to smooth it out.*

Acknowledgments

Main Literature Selections

"Abuelita's Lap" from *Confetti: Poems for Children*, by Pat Mora. Text copyright ©1996 by Pat Mora. Reprinted by permission of Lee & Low Books, Inc.

Excerpt from *Ah, Music!* by Aliki. Copyright ©2003 by Aliki Brandenberg. Reprinted by permission of HarperCollins Publishers.

Animals Building Homes by Wendy Perkins. Copyright ©2004 by Capstone Press. All rights reserved. Reprinted by permission of Capstone Press Publishers.

Click, Clack, Moo: Cows That Type by Doreen Cronin, illustrated by Betsy Lewin. Text copyright ©2000 by Doreen Cronin. Illustrations copyright ©2000 by Betsy Lewin. Reprinted by permission of Simon & Schuster's Books for Young Readers, an Imprint of Simon & Schuster's Children's Publishing Division. All rights reserved.

Diary of a Spider by Doreen Cronin, illustrated by Harry Bliss. Text copyright ©2005 by Doreen Cronin. Illustrations copyright ©2005 by Harry Bliss. Reprinted by permission of HarperCollins Children's Books, a division of HarperCollins Publishers, and Pippin Properties, Inc.

Dogs by Jennifer Blizin Gillis. Text copyright ©2004. Reprinted by permission of Heinemann Library.

"Everybody Says" from *Everything and Anything* by Dorothy Aldis, copyright ©1925-1927, renewed 1953-1955 by Dorothy Aldis. Reprinted by permission of G.P. Putnam's Sons, A Division of Penguin Young Readers Group, A Member of Penguin Group (USA) Inc. All rights reserved.

"Grandpa's Stories" by Langston Hughes from *The Collected Poems of Langston Hughes* by Arnold Rampersal with David Roessel, Associate Editor. Copyright ©1994 by The Estate of Langston Hughes. Reprinted by permission of Alfred A. Knopf, a division of Random House, Inc. and Harold Ober Associates Incorporated.

Helen Keller by Jane Sutcliffe, illustrated by Elaine Verstraete. Text copyright ©2002 by Jane Sutcliffe. Illustrations copyright © 2002 by Elaine Verstraete. All rights reserved. Reprinted by permission of Carolrhoda Books Inc., a division of Lerner Publishing Group, Inc.

Henry and Mudge: The First Book by Cynthia Rylant, illustrated by Suçie Stevenson. Text copyright ©1987 by Cynthia Rylant. Illustrations copyright ©1997 by Suçie Stevenson. Reprinted by permission of Simon & Schuster's Books for Young Readers, an imprint of Simon & Schuster Children's Publishing Division. All rights reserved.

How Chipmunk Got His Stripes by Joseph and James Bruchac, illustrated by José Aruego & Ariane Dewey. Text copyright ©2001 by Joseph Bruchac and James Bruchac. Illustrations copyright ©2001 by José Aruego and Ariane Dewey. All rights reserved. Published by permission of Dial Books for Young Readers, a member of Penguin Books for Young Readers, a division of Penguin Group (USA) Inc.

Jellies: The Life of Jellyfish by Twig C. George. Text copyright ©2000 by Twig C. George. All rights reserved. Reprinted by permission of Millbrook Press, a division of Lerner Publishing Group, and Curtis Brown, Ltd.

Mi Familia/My Family by George Ancona, children's drawings by Camila Carballo, photographs by George Ancona. Text copyright ©2004 by George Ancona. Children's drawings copyright ©2004 by Camila Carballo. Photographs copyright ©2004 by George Ancona. All rights reserved. Reprinted by permission of Children's Press, an imprint of Scholastic Library Publishing, Inc.

Officer Buckle and Gloria written and illustrated by Peggy Rathmann. Text and illustrations copyright ©1995 by Peggy Rathmann. All rights reserved. Reprinted by permission of G. P. Putnam's Sons, a division of Penguin Putnam Books for Young Readers, a division of Penguin Group (USA) Inc., and Sheldon Fogelman Agency, Inc.

Cover illustration from *Poppleton in Winter* by Cynthia Rylant. Illustrations by Mark Teague. Illustration copyright ©2001 by Mark Teague. Reprinted by permission of Scholastic Inc. SCHOLASTIC'S Material shall not be published, retransmitted, broadcast, downloaded, modified or adapted (rewritten), manipulated, reproduced or otherwise distributed and/or exploited in any way without the prior written authorization of Scholastic Inc.

Schools Around the World by Margaret C. Hall. Originally published as Schools. Text copyright ©2002 Heinemann Library. Reprinted by permission of Heinemann Library, a division of

Credits

Photo Credits

Placement Key: (r) right, (l) left, (c) center, (t) top, (b) bottom, (bg) background

2 (cl) Tony Taylor / San Antonio Zoo; **2** (cl) ©George Ancona; **2** (bl) Digital Vision/Alamy; **3** (tc) ©George Doyle/Getty Images; **3** (tl) Don Farrall/Getty Images; **4** (tc) Erwin & Peggy Bauer/Wildstock; **4** (tl) ©INTERFOTO/Alamy Images; **4** (tl) ©Jim Zipp/Photo Researchers, Inc.; **4** (tl) ©SuperStock/Alamy Images; **4** (tl) ©Juniors Bildarchiv/Alamy Images; **4** (cl) ©Justin Sullivan/Staff/Getty Images; **4** (bc) Kul Bhatia/Photo Researchers, Inc.; **4** (bl) ©Terry Vine/Getty Images; **5** (cl) Comstock Images / Getty Images; **5** (cl) ©Poelzer Wolfgang/Alamy Images; **6** (tl) The Alex Foundation; **6** (bl) ©Joshua Hodge Photography/Getty Images; **6** (bl) © David Buffington/Photodisc/Getty Images; **6** (bl) © Getty Images/Digital Vision; **6** (tl) Najlah Feanny/Corbis; Blind [**9**] ©Andy Sacks/Getty Images; **10** (b) Jerry Shulman/Superstock; **10** (t) Arco Images GmbH/Alamy; **10** (tr) Tony Taylor / San Antonio Zoo; **11** (cl) Blickwinkel/Alamy; **11** (tr) Dave Stamboulis/Alamy; **11** (br) ©Alamy Images; **11** (tl) Getty Images; **11** (bl) David Burton/Alamy; **12** ©Big Cheese Photo LLC/Alamy; **27** (t) ©Stockdisc/Getty Images; **28** (b) Artville / Getty Images; **30** (b) Tony Taylor / San Antonio Zoo; **30** (tl) Tony Taylor / San Antonio Zoo; **31** (tl) Scott Doll/San Antonio Zoo; **31** (cr) Gandee Vasan/Getty Images; **31** (br) GK Hart/Vikki Hart/Photodisc/Getty Images; **32** San Antonio Zoo; **32** (b) GK Hart/Vikki Hart/Getty Images; **33** (t) ©Photodisc/Getty Images; **33** (b) Tony Taylor / San Antonio Zoo; **33** (tr) Tony Taylor / San Antonio Zoo; **37** (br) Exactostock / SuperStock; **38** (t) Edgardo Contreras/Getty; **38** (b) MoMo Productions/Getty; **38** (tc) Digital Vision/Alamy; **38** (tl) ©George Ancona; **39** (tr) ©Kwame Zikomo/Purestock/Getty Images; **39** (tl) Exactostock/Superstock; **39** (cl) Tom Stewart/Corbis; **39** (cr) David Young-Wolff/PhotoEdit; **39** (bl) Ronnie Kaufman/Age Fotostock America, Inc.; **39** (br) Masterfile; **40** ©George Ancona; **41** ©Stockbroker/Alamy Images; **42** ©George Ancona; **42** (tl) ©George Ancona; **43** ©George Ancona; **44** (t) ©George Ancona; **44** (cl) ©George Ancona; **45** (t) ©George Ancona; **46** (bl) ©George Ancona; **46** (r) ©George Ancona; **47** (t) ©George Ancona; **49** ©George Ancona; **50** (tl) ©George Ancona; **50** (r) ©George Ancona; **50** (cl) ©George Ancona; **51** (b) ©George Ancona; **51** (t) ©George Ancona; **52** ©George Ancona; **53** (l) ©George Ancona; **53** (r) ©George Ancona; **55** ©George Ancona; **56** ©George Ancona; **58** ©George Ancona; **59** ©BananaStock/Getty Images; **61** (b) BananaStock / Jupiterimages; **61** (tl) ©George Ancona; **62** (b) Stockbyte/Alamy; **62** (tl) Digital Vision/Alamy; **63** (tr) ©Jack Hollingsworth/Photodisc/Getty Images; **64** (b) Digital Vision/Alamy; **64** (br) Digital Vision/Alamy; **65** (t) ©Image Source/Getty Images; **65** (cr) ©Exactostock/Superstock; **65** (tr) Digital Vision/Alamy; **70** (tr) ©Artville/Getty Images; **70** (br) ©JupiterImages/i2i/Alamy Images; **70** (tc) Don Farrall/Getty Images; **70** (tl) ©George Doyle/Getty Images; **71** (cl) ©Glow Wellness/Getty Images; **71** (cr) ©Lightly Salted/Alamy Images; **71** (br) ©HMH; **72** (tl) ©George Doyle/Getty Images; **73** ©Life on white/Alamy Images; **74** (tl) ©George Doyle/Getty Images; **75** ©George Doyle/Getty Images; **76** (tl) Getty Images/Photodisc; **76** (bl) ©Ingram Publishing/Alamy Images; **76** (r) ©GK Hart/Vikki Hart/Getty Images; **79** (br) Coneyl Jay/Stone/Getty Images;